The GOURMET Galley

The
G O U R M E T
Galley
FINE COOKING ON SMALL BOATS

TERENCE JANERICCO

INTERNATIONAL MARINE
PUBLISHING COMPANY
Camden, Maine 04843

©1986 by International Marine Publishing Company

Typeset by Typeworks, Belfast, Maine
Printed and bound by BookCrafters, Inc., Chelsea, Michigan

Published by International Marine Publishing Company
21 Elm Street, Camden, Maine 04843
(207) 236-4342

Library of Congress Cataloging in Publication Data

Janericco, Terence.
    The gourmet galley.

    1. Cookery, Marine.   I. Title.
TX840.M7J36   1986   641.5'753   86-10602
ISBN 0-87742-224-9

TO DAVID CIUNYK
SINCERE THANKS FOR ALLOWING ME
TO TEST THESE RECIPES ON HIS BOATS,
THE TANKA AND THE TANKA II.

TO ROBERT EHRLICH
FOR ALLOWING ME TO SAIL
WITHOUT TESTING ANY RECIPES.

CONTENTS

ACKNOWLEDGMENTS

My thanks to Glenna Bradley for her care and concern in typing the various drafts of this book. To the patience of my editor, Jon Eaton, who has handled my hurricanes of temper with the calm of a windless sea. Finally, but not least, to Beverly Heinle, a steadfast agent who has listened to my complaints and frustrations with good humor.

PREFACE

When it comes to cooking and eating on a boat, my fellow sailors intrigue me. Truly, owners and crews of pleasure craft live above the poverty level – usually well above it. On land, they dine in the best restaurants and prepare delicious, creative food to serve their guests at home. But put them within a mind's eye view of a boat and they lose all sense of taste, ability to entertain, and reasonable care for their own gustatory well-being. The same people who would turn a restaurant into the "Wreck of the Hesperus" over a poorly made sauce suddenly feel that there is a pride and pleasure gained from eating soggy sandwiches and canned goods that even the manufacturer is ashamed of.

I suspect that part of this has to do with the fact that many sailors equate the "bounding main" with a life of leisure, which all too often translates into no cooking or a minimum of cooking. Sometimes these are people who rarely cook or cook only under extreme duress, which is fine for them. For many of us, however, cooking is a pleasure, a treat, a therapy, a joy, without which we feel deprived. Still, even we at times sink to the depths when faced with a galley. Yet, good food does not have to take hours of preparation. It is not necessary to slave over a hot stove to prepare truly delicious, creative dishes. A little thought and careful planning are all that is required to produce good, flavorful food.

I hope that this book will not only give you specific recipes to guide you in preparing wonderful meals in short order, but will also encourage you to develop your own ideas for wonderful meals.

Galley facilities differ greatly from boat to boat. They can consist of no more than a tiny hibachi on the fantail to a full kitchen with freezer, dishwasher, and processor. Indeed, large ocean liners have full professional kitchens with space for an army of chefs. Most of my sailing has been done on boats in the 22- to 45-foot category, and it is in those galleys that I have practiced cooking for this book. Initially, like many others, I felt that it was mandatory to use canned foods. My palate soon rebelled. I started to plan menus ahead and prepare for a cruise so that I could serve superior food. I searched through books for guidance and found too often that they did not suit my needs. They used too many canned goods, and too often the recipes were cute rather than actually appetizing. Therefore, I set to work on a book of delicious, easily prepared dishes suitable for any occasion, but written specifically with small-boat facilities in mind.

March 1985
Eastry House
St. Peter's Parish
Barbados

ONE

INTRODUCTION

Before you can start to cook, you must have something in which to cook. Unfortunately, the galley of a boat often becomes the receptacle for discarded cookware from home. The pots and pans that no longer work there are expected to work in more difficult conditions. I recommend that you consider the galley as seriously as any other area of the boat. Decent food can make or break a cruise. Why take chances with the wrong equipment or just poor-quality equipment? There are a few practical matters to consider. For instance, tin- or nickel-lined copper is wonderful at home, but too expensive and too hard to maintain at sea. No one wants to spend his or her time polishing copper pans. Brightwork, maybe, but not pots and pans. I suggest that the most useful pans to buy are the coated aluminum ones that have been on the market for the last several years. The gray coating always looks good, and the surface, though not stickproof, will season to an almost nonstick surface. It can, however, be scoured without damaging the metal. These pans are lightweight yet durable.

You do not need a lot of pans. A couple of skillets (a 6-inch skillet for cooking a single order of eggs or hamburger or for reheating a leftover vegetable, and a 9-inch skillet for general sautéing) should do. Your inventory should also include two or three saucepans of ½- to 2-quart capacity, a large kettle for cooking lobsters and clams and making soups, a 3-quart saucepan for soups, and perhaps a wok. If you get a wok, make sure that it measures a good 14 inches across and that it comes with a flat bottom. Wooden handles are another important safety feature. The wok is very versatile and can be used to stir fry or steam vegetables, chicken, or seafood – including lobsters and clams. It can even serve as the dishpan.

In addition to pans, the recipes in this book also make use of the following baking equipment: a cookie sheet, 9x13-inch baking pan, shallow baking pan, and Dutch oven. The real point is not to have too many pans; otherwise you will spend a lot of time washing up when you should be enjoying yourself.

A few other items you will need are a good-sized colander, a four-sided grater, a decent cooking fork, and a couple of wooden spoons. I am always in favor of a good wire whisk or two, preferably with a good handle so that you can get a full grip, rather than one of those with twisted wire. Ideally, one whisk should fit comfortably in a 1-quart saucepan without falling out and the other should fit in a 3-quart pan.

Knives are crucial. No matter where you cook. If they are not good, you will use too much effort to perform the simplest tasks. I recommend that you buy very good knives of hardened steel with a high carbon content so that you can sharpen them yourself. You should be able to prepare any of the recipes in this book with a paring knife and an 8- to 10-inch chef's knife. You may want a bread knife and a filleting knife as well. Finally, have a sharpening steel on hand so that you can keep the edge on the knives. Of course, you will make it clear that these items are for cooking. Let the captain go buy his or her own knife to splice lines, etc.

GUIDE TO SUCCESSFUL GALLEY COOKING

Prepare a set of menus to cover all the meals to be eaten on your cruise in the same careful manner that your navigator plans the day's sail.

Plan your menus so that the food that will spoil first is served first. If you are going to be at sea for a week or more, plan dishes using lettuce and other delicate vegetables for the first few days, and save the cauliflower, carrots, and other sturdier vegetables for the end of the week.

Freeze any meats that are not to be used in the first day or two. They can substitute for some of the ice and will keep "fresh" until you are prepared to serve them. Make sure that you use meats in the order that they are likely to thaw. For example, use ground meats before unground, cut up before whole, and poultry before red meats.

Some canned goods are called for in these recipes, but very few. These are items that taste as good canned as they do fresh, such as beets; that form a base for other ingredients, such as stock; or that taste good in their own right, such as bacon or nuts.

Be sure to have the spices and seasonings that you will need. These will vary from cook to cook. Some prefer the subtleties of tarragon, chervil, and chives, while others think cayenne, coriander, and cumin make the world go around. Check over your list of ingredients carefully so that you will have what you need when you need it. It is difficult to pick up a bottle of Chinese chili oil at a dockside market, for example, unless your dockside is Kowloon harbor.

One problem at sea is salt. The refined table salt most people use has a tendency to stick and clog the saltshaker. Certainly, having rice in the shaker does help, but I recommend using kosher salt. It does not clog up, but also does not fit into a saltshaker. I use a saltbox, but any small covered container would do. There is no substitute for freshly ground pepper. Get a good peppermill. The working parts of peppermills are often not well made and do not grind the pepper evenly. Try them out in the store before you buy.

Use fresh garlic and onions whenever you are cooking. Do not be tempted to use dried or freeze-dried substitutes. The flavor is not the same and, in fact, is rather offensive. A couple of heads of garlic and a bag or two of onions will store easily and will last the length of your voyage. If some should spoil or you end up wasting part of an onion, the financial loss is too small to be worth considering.

Bear in mind at which ports you will moor and when. If you stop every evening, your menus can be quite different than if you are at sea the whole time. Check the facilities listed for each port. Some general stores may not carry elaborate ingredients, but you can almost always find lettuce, tomatoes, potatoes, onions, and a limited selection of meats. Of course, you have to moor early enough to go shopping. If you dock at 9:00 p.m. and leave at 6:00 a.m., you will probably find stores closed.

If you are going to stop every night, or every other night, at a port with reasonable facilities, you need not stock up on perishables. Buy the things you need when you want to cook them.

But enough of this. No one can tell you how to organize your galley or what to stock. Your likes and dislikes will determine your choice of supplies. Use the recipes and suggestions in this book to guide you to good, easy cooking. Then you will have plenty of time to relax and enjoy the salt air and the glorious sun, which is the reason you went sailing in the first place.

I believe that every cook has the inalienable right to say no. There should be a meal for which you feel no responsibility. For me, it is breakfast. I will make coffee and share it. The rest is up to the others, including the cleaning up. This rule is inviolable, and anyone who tries to get me to break it is in trouble. A good friend, Alice, does not do lunch. She ignores it with impunity. That is the time she chooses to be on deck enjoying the sail, not cooking. She assigns another crewmember to prepare lunch or leaves everyone to his or her own devices. To avoid possible disasters and accusations, she does make it clear what is to be used for lunch and what she is planning to use for another meal. We both make sure that we have provided the ingredients for the meals we do not prepare.

One final point: remember to take this book with you. Careful menu planning and shopping will come to naught if you leave the recipes at home, unless you have a spectacular memory. (Truly smart readers will buy two copies, one for use at home and one at sea.)

TWO

APPETIZERS AND HORS D'OEUVRES

There are all sorts of prepared foods to serve with a cocktail. Many of the canned foods, in fact, are extremely good and certainly worth considering. If you are not sure of a product, try it before you go. Herring in mustard sauce may thrill me, but you might find it less than delightful. When you are hungry and short on supplies, it is tragic to try something for the first time, expecting it to be wonderful, only to be disappointed.

Potato chips and crackers can be stand-bys on board a boat. They are the quick, junk-food snack (especially potato chips) that we all complain about but at times enjoy greatly. Chips and crackers can often be purchased in sturdy, resealable containers. If not, start to collect such containers, especially for crackers, which get limp so quickly. I keep a number of old cracker tins around for just this purpose, but there are many types of plastic containers that will do just as well. I repack my favorite brand of hand-fried potato chips in sturdy, sealable containers, rather than buy chips made from potato flakes or the often oversalted commercial brands.

Nuts are often sold in sturdy, resealable containers. They are a convenient snack food that is also nutritious, which should help to ease the guilt of those who worry about their diets.

Crackers come in a wide variety of flavors and thicknesses. A cruise can be a fun time to sample some of the more exotic types. Occasionally, there are cheese-filled crackers that taste delicious rather than artificial. Be sure to find a favorite before taking up any storage space, to avoid disappointment.

Crackers and chips can be served with spreads or dips, which can be made from leftovers, canned fish, a little flavoring, mayonnaise, cream cheese, or sour cream. Although I give specific recipes, do not feel that you must follow them exactly. If the recipe calls for tuna fish and you have shrimp, crab, or smoked oysters, it will still work. It will just taste different. The small amount of leftover fish that is really not enough for one person as a main course can be treated as above and turned into a delicious spread. Add cayenne pepper, lemon juice, minced dill pickles, or capers to make it piquant and interesting. Plan to use what you have on board as creatively as possible.

Leftovers are a wonderful source of cocktail food. They allow you to make full use of food rather than throw it away, and to rework it so that it is interesting and no longer just a leftover. Use a little thought and a small amount of effort. The unfinished steak or lamb chop that is not enough for another meal can be cubed and marinated in a vinaigrette for anywhere from a few minutes to an hour. Serve it with toothpicks.

Leftover string beans, carrots, and other vegetables can also be tossed in a vinaigrette to be served with drinks or as part of a luncheon salad. Those mush-rooms that just might make it until you are ready to cook them can be preserved in a vinaigrette for another day or so.

A few words about vinaigrette: Vinaigrette in its simplest form consists of oil and vinegar with salt and pepper. You can elaborate on it by adding some herbs, a bit of crushed garlic, perhaps a pinch of cayenne, or a dash of Tabasco for a perky finish, or crumble in blue cheese or mix in grated Parmesan. I almost always add mustard in varying quantities. Vinaigrette is ready within a few seconds and is always fresh. My recipe is on page 178. Remember, it is much easier to stow a large bottle of olive oil and a small bottle of vinegar or a few lemons than to stow four or five bottles of commercial salad dressing. Your own dressing will not taste of chemicals, and what you make will be much better than any dressing you can buy, with virtually no effort on your part.

Cheeses, of course, are a popular appetizer. Buy according to the amount of time you plan to spend at sea. Firm cheeses like cheddars or Gruyère will last several weeks in a cool place. Any mold can be wiped off with a cloth dipped in vinegar. Brie and Camembert can be brought on board fresh, but should be eaten within the first few days. For emergencies, keep a few cans of canned Camembert or Brie. They keep a long time, and though not as good as fresh, they are quite edible. You can improve the flavor of a canned Brie, for instance, by warming it in a pie plate over low heat on a hibachi or in an oven and serving it as a warm dip or spread with crackers. Or mash the cheese, rind and all, with some crushed garlic and perhaps some tarragon, chervil, or other herb. For more spice, sprinkle generously with freshly ground black pepper.

There are dozens of kinds of canned fish, plain or in preparations, that can be turned into choice tidbits with a little imagination. Some, such as smoked clams, mussels, or oysters, can be served as they are with lemon wedges. In a recipe, feel free to interchange any of these. They can be chopped or mashed, flavored with minced onion, blended into cream cheese or sour cream, or bound with a little mayonnaise as a dip or spread. Add a little lemon juice or tomato paste for a more piquant flavor.

Unfortunately, most canned meats are not very good. Bacon is the only exception that comes to mind. Other meats tend to be too salty. Dried chipped beef can be chopped up, mixed with minced onion, crushed garlic, and a dash of Worcestershire sauce, and blended with cream cheese or sour cream as a spread or dip. Remember that the beef is very salty, so use salt sparingly. Canned hams are also useful to have on board, but the smaller hams tend to be made of the less choice portions of ham. Try a couple of brands before you choose the one you want to stock.

There is a good selection of cured meats that hold up well on a boat. Go to your local delicatessen and buy a variety of so-called hard salamis, such as pepperoni, Genoa, Jewish, or Abbruzzese. Store in the ice chest to serve wrapped around a strip of cream cheese or a pickled carrot or green bean. The slices can be served on their own or with cheeses or fruits. If you buy whole sections of salamis, you can cut them into cubes, rather than paper-thin slices, and spear them on toothpicks with grapes, strawberries, or pineapple wedges. Melon, of course, works wonderfully with thin slices of salami. Cubes of salami can be mixed with scrambled eggs or tossed into an omelette. Use them to add zest to a tomato sauce for pasta or to add interest to a salad. At most ports you will find a store with a selection of cold cuts that you can serve as an hors d'oeuvre. Your best bet for meat hors d'ouevres is to use leftovers. Chop the extra chicken leg into fine dice and mix it with a touch of curry and mayonnaise to spread on crackers. Cut strips of chicken breast and dip the ends into a spicy mayonnaise flavored with hot pepper sauce, or make a simple salad.

Vegetables work well, whether with a simple dip, or marinated leftovers. Use some common sense. You cannot marinate leftover mashed potatoes. (Why would you mash potatoes on a boat?) If you do have leftover mashed potatoes, mix them with a generous amount of crushed garlic and a small jar of mashed pimientos and blend well. Season with vinegar, salt, pepper, and olive oil to taste, then serve as a spread. Rice does not make a good appetizer, but it can be reheated as a stuffing for chops, turned into extender with a variety of vegetables, and made into a rice salad to serve for luncheon.

Sometimes leftovers are just that. If no one wants to eat them the next day and you cannot think of a way to serve them as appetizers, realize that their life is ended. Send them overboard.

A friend of mine goes to various ethnic markets to pick up a selection of foods that she can serve as appetizers on board: canned pâtés, sausages, fish preparations such as sardines in various sauces, herring in sauces, stuffed grape leaves, caponata (the Italian eggplant spread), tahini, and hummus, for example. She keeps a well-stocked larder not only on board, but also at home.

The point, as always, is to use your imagination. Look at the market shelves with greater interest than usual. See what is readily available and what you can enhance with a little bit of effort. If it takes hours of preparation, scratch it. Remember that you are supposed to be enjoying this. Your time should be devoted more to main courses. If you spend all of your time on the hors d'oeuvres, you will run out of steam before dinner. Try the recipes below for quick hors d'oeuvres, so you can keep everyone happy while getting more serious things done or so you can sit on the deck, sip a gin and tonic, and watch that glorious sunset.

Spiced Vegetable Dip

☐ In a bowl, mix the sour cream, lemon juice, Worcestershire sauce, onion, celery salt, garlic, and Tabasco sauce. Let stand for at least 30 minutes for the flavors to meld.

☐ Use as a dip for vegetables, corn chips, or potato chips. Can be used as a sauce for leftover vegetables.

YIELDS 2 ¼ CUPS.

INGREDIENTS:
1 PINT SOUR CREAM
1 TABLESPOON LEMON JUICE
1 TABLESPOON WORCESTER-
SHIRE SAUCE
2 TEASPOONS MINCED ONION
1 ½ TEASPOONS CELERY SALT
¼ TEASPOON CRUSHED
GARLIC
¼ TEASPOON TABASCO
SAUCE

Sour Cream Dill Sauce

☐ In a bowl, combine the sour cream and dill and mix well. Season with salt and pepper.

☐ Serve chilled, or warm in a double boiler – do not let it boil. Serve with raw vegetables, crackers, or chips as a dip. Can be used as a sauce for hot or cold poached fish or for broiled fish. Can also be used as a dressing for chicken or fish salad.

YIELDS 1 ¼ CUPS.

INGREDIENTS:
1 CUP SOUR CREAM
½ CUP MINCED DILL
SALT AND PEPPER TO TASTE

Sauce Tunisienne

INGREDIENTS:

1½ CUPS TOMATOES, PEELED,
   SEEDED, AND CHOPPED
⅓ CUP OLIVE OIL
¼ CUP MINCED PARSLEY
1½ TABLESPOONS MINCED
   SCALLIONS
2 GARLIC CLOVES, MINCED
½ TEASPOON CRUSHED RED
   PEPPER
½ TEASPOON GROUND
   CORIANDER
¼ TEASPOON SUGAR
SALT AND PEPPER TO TASTE
1 CUP SOUR CREAM
   (OPTIONAL)

□ In a bowl, combine the tomatoes, olive oil, parsley, scallions, garlic, crushed red pepper, ground coriander, and sugar, and season with salt and pepper to taste. Add sour cream, if desired.

□ Serve the sauce without the sour cream with broiled scallops, shrimps, pork chops, lamb steaks, or hamburgers.

□ Add the sour cream and use as a dip for vegetables or chips.

YIELDS 2 TO 3 CUPS.

Chili Dipping Sauce

INGREDIENTS:

3 TOMATOES, PEELED,
   SEEDED, AND CHOPPED
3 CANNED GREEN CHILIES,
   MINCED
1 GARLIC CLOVE, MINCED
1 TEASPOON LEMON JUICE
SALT AND PEPPER TO TASTE

□ In a bowl, combine the tomatoes, chilies, garlic, lemon juice, salt, and pepper. Let stand for at least 30 minutes for flavors to meld.

□ Use as a dip for crackers or corn chips, or as a sauce for broiled fish, hamburgers, or pork chops.

YIELDS 1½ CUPS.

Sauce Horcher

☐ In a medium bowl, beat the egg yolks, mustard, and vinegar until they start to thicken. Pour in the oil in droplets until it thickens, then add the oil in a slow, steady stream, beating constantly, until it is incorporated and the mixture is thickened.

☐ Add the Cognac, chili sauce, lemon juice, celery, horseradish, shallots, chives, and parsley. Blend to combine.

☐ Use as a dip for shrimp, scallops, or crab claws. Serve with broiled steak. Leftovers can be used as a salad dressing.

YIELDS 1½ CUPS.

INGREDIENTS:

3 EGG YOLKS

1½ TEASPOONS DRY MUSTARD

2 TABLESPOONS WINE VINEGAR

1 CUP OLIVE OIL

2 TABLESPOONS COGNAC

2 TABLESPOONS CHILI SAUCE

2 TABLESPOONS LEMON JUICE

2 TABLESPOONS MINCED CELERY

2 TABLESPOONS GRATED HORSERADISH

2 TABLESPOONS MINCED SHALLOTS

1 TABLESPOON MINCED CHIVES

1 TABLESPOON MINCED PARSLEY

Curry Dipping Sauce

☐ In a bowl, mix the mayonnaise, sour cream, curry powder, soy sauce, salt, and pepper together. Let flavors meld for at least 30 minutes.

☐ Serve as a dipping sauce for vegetables. Can be used as an accompaniment to broiled fish.

YIELDS 2 CUPS.

INGREDIENTS:

1 CUP MAYONNAISE, SEE PAGE 178

1 CUP SOUR CREAM

1 TEASPOON CURRY POWDER

½ TEASPOON SOY SAUCE

SALT AND PEPPER TO TASTE

Guacamole

INGREDIENTS:

1 RIPE AVOCADO, PEELED
AND SEEDED

1 TO 2 GREEN CHILIES,
CHOPPED

2 TABLESPOONS LIME JUICE

SALT TO TASTE

1 TOMATO, PEELED, SEEDED,
AND CHOPPED

☐ In a bowl, mash the avocado pulp until coarse, and beat in the chilies, lime juice, salt, and tomatoes.

☐ Arrange in a bowl and serve within an hour. To try to keep the guacamole from turning dark, insert the pit from the avocado into the middle of the mixture.

☐ Serve with crackers, corn chips, or vegetables, or use as a sauce for broiled fish or baked potatoes.

YIELDS ABOUT ¾ CUP.

Avocado Horseradish Dip

INGREDIENTS:

1 LARGE RIPE AVOCADO,
PEELED

½ CUP SOUR CREAM

2 TABLESPOONS GRATED
HORSERADISH

2 TEASPOONS MINCED ONION

SALT AND PEPPER TO TASTE

TABASCO SAUCE TO TASTE

PAPRIKA

☐ In a bowl, mash the avocado with a fork until fairly smooth. Add the sour cream, horseradish, onion, salt, pepper, and Tabasco. Arrange in a bowl and sprinkle with paprika.

☐ Serve as a dip for cold cooked shrimp, scallops, or broiled fish. Can also be used as a dip for crackers, corn chips, or potato chips.

YIELDS ABOUT 1¼ CUPS.

Marinated Carrots

- ☐ Cook the carrot sticks in boiling salted water until just barely tender. Drain.

- ☐ In a bowl, combine the oil, vinegar, onion, garlic, basil, salt and pepper. Add carrots and toss gently.

- ☐ Keep chilled, covered for 12 hours, tossing occasionally.

- ☐ Serve the sticks arranged on salad greens, sprinkled with lemon juice. For cocktails, arrange in a cup surrounded by lemon wedges, if desired.

YIELDS ABOUT 3 CUPS.

INGREDIENTS:
6 TO 8 CARROTS, PEELED
    AND CUT INTO STICKS
½ CUP OLIVE OIL
¼ CUP WHITE WINE VINEGAR
1 SMALL ONION, SLICED
2 GARLIC CLOVES, PEELED
1 TEASPOON DRIED BASIL
SALT TO TASTE
½ TEASPOON PEPPER
SALAD GREENS (OPTIONAL)
JUICE OF 1 LARGE LEMON

Marinated Mushrooms

This not only works as an hors d'oeuvre, but is a way to preserve mushrooms that have been around for a while. Drained and minced, they can be used as a stuffing for tomatoes or as an accompaniment to mashed potatoes. Whole, they are a popular hors d'oeuvre.

- ☐ Wash mushrooms quickly, drain, and remove stems if necessary. Set aside in bowl or plastic container with a lid.

- ☐ In a saucepan, simmer the lemon juice, salt, vinegar, olive oil, garlic, thyme, parsley, bay leaf, peppercorns, and coriander seeds for 20 minutes.

- ☐ Pour over the mushrooms and marinate for anywhere from 6 hours up to 3 days.

YIELDS ABOUT 3 CUPS.

INGREDIENTS:
1 POUND SMALL MUSHROOMS
JUICE OF ½ LEMON
SALT TO TASTE
8 TABLESPOONS WINE
    VINEGAR
8 TABLESPOONS OLIVE OIL
1 TO 2 CLOVES GARLIC,
    CRUSHED
1 SPRIG THYME
2 SPRIGS PARSLEY
1 BAY LEAF
5 PEPPERCORNS
10 CORIANDER SEEDS

Bibelkäse

INGREDIENTS:

2 CUPS SMALL CURD
  COTTAGE CHEESE
½ CUP HEAVY CREAM
1 TABLESPOON MINCED
  PARSLEY
3 GARLIC CLOVES, MINCED
SALT AND PEPPER TO TASTE

☐ Sieve the cottage cheese into a bowl. Beat in the cream, parsley, garlic, salt, and pepper.

☐ Let stand for at least 30 minutes for flavors to meld. Can be kept chilled for 2 to 3 days.

YIELDS ABOUT 2½ CUPS.

Beer Cheese Spread

INGREDIENTS:

2 CUPS GRATED CHEDDAR
  CHEESE
¼ CUP BUTTER
2 TEASPOONS DIJON
  MUSTARD
2 TEASPOONS MINCED
  SHALLOTS
½ TEASPOON ANCHOVY
  PASTE
½ TEASPOON CARAWAY SEED
PINCH OF CAYENNE PEPPER
¼ CUP BEER

☐ In a bowl, beat the cheese, butter, mustard, shallots, anchovy paste, caraway seeds, and cayenne pepper together. Gradually beat in the beer and beat until fluffy.

☐ Can be kept chilled for up to 4 days.

☐ Vary the flavor by omitting the anchovy paste and caraway seed and adding ½ teaspoon ground sage, or by omitting caraway seed and adding 1 tablespoon poppy seeds.

YIELDS ABOUT 2½ CUPS.

Diablotins

INGREDIENTS:

6 OUNCES GRATED GRUYÈRE
2 EGGS, LIGHTLY BEATEN
DASH OF PAPRIKA
DASH OF CAYENNE PEPPER
4 SLICES BREAD, TOASTED

☐ Preheat the oven to 400°F.

☐ In a bowl, mix the cheese, eggs, paprika, and cayenne pepper. Spread on the toast.

☐ Bake for 15 minutes or until the cheese is bubbly. Cut into triangles.

YIELDS 16 TOASTS.

Herb Cheese Spread

☐ In a bowl, beat the cream cheese, parsley, chives, cream, salt, and pepper until fluffy. Pack into a container and use as a spread.

☐ If you have adequate refrigeration, chill until firm and shape into marble-sized balls. For color and added flavor, roll the balls in paprika, minced parsley, poppy seeds, or toasted sesame seeds.

YIELDS ABOUT ¾ CUP.

INGREDIENTS:

3 OUNCES CREAM CHEESE, SOFTENED

2 TABLESPOONS MINCED PARSLEY

2 TABLESPOONS MINCED CHIVES

1 TABLESPOON HEAVY CREAM

SALT AND PEPPER TO TASTE

Brazil Nut–Clam Spread

☐ In a bowl, beat the cream cheese and curry powder together until smooth.

☐ Drain the clams of any juices and stir into the cream cheese with the nuts. Serve with crackers.

☐ If fresh-cooked clams are not available, substitute a 10-ounce can of minced clams. Of course, only when you are sailing in the Great Lakes will this happen.

YIELDS ABOUT ¾ CUP.

INGREDIENTS:

3 OUNCES CREAM CHEESE

PINCH OF CURRY POWDER

1 CUP MINCED COOKED CLAMS

¼ CUP MINCED BRAZIL NUTS

Herbed Garlic Cheese

INGREDIENTS:

½ POUND CREAM CHEESE, SOFTENED

1 TO 2 TABLESPOONS HEAVY CREAM

1 TO 2 TABLESPOONS MINCED PARSLEY

1 GARLIC CLOVE, MINCED

1 TEASPOON DRIED MARJORAM

1 TEASPOON DRIED OREGANO

1 TEASPOON SAVORY

SALT TO TASTE

☐ In a bowl, beat the cream with the cheese until soft and smooth. Beat in the parsley, garlic, marjoram, oregano, and savory, and season to taste with the salt.

☐ Chill for an hour or more for flavors to meld. Will keep, chilled, for at least 2 days.

☐ If desired, change the herbs to suit what you have on hand or can get fresh. Omit the savory and add rosemary, sage, or basil. Omit the marjoram, oregano, and savory and use chives, chervil, and tarragon.

☐ Use the leftover as a quick sauce for pasta. Serve with freshly ground black pepper.

YIELDS ABOUT 1½ CUPS.

Herbed Toasts

INGREDIENTS:

½ CUP SOFT BUTTER

¼ TEASPOON MINCED PARSLEY

¼ TEASPOON MINCED TARRAGON

¼ TEASPOON MINCED CHERVIL

¼ TEASPOON MINCED CHIVES

SALT AND PEPPER TO TASTE

⅛ TEASPOON CRUSHED GARLIC

18 THIN SLICES OF BREAD

☐ Preheat oven to 350°F.

☐ In a bowl, mash the butter until soft, and beat in the parsley, tarragon, chervil, chives, salt, pepper, and garlic.

☐ Spread on the bread slices and bake until golden and crisp. Cut into strips or squares.

YIELDS 54 TO 72 TOASTS.

Cheddar Cheese and Olive Balls

☐ In a bowl, mix the cheese, olives, butter, garlic, Tabasco sauce, and cayenne pepper together. Form into one large ball or about 18 small balls.

☐ Any leftover can be used as a topping for broiled hamburgers.

YIELDS ABOUT 2 CUPS.

INGREDIENTS:
1 POUND CHEDDAR CHEESE, GRATED
½ CUP CHOPPED RIPE OLIVES
4 TABLESPOONS BUTTER
1 GARLIC CLOVE, MINCED
TABASCO SAUCE TO TASTE
CAYENNE PEPPER TO TASTE

Sardine Spread

☐ In a bowl, beat the cream cheese until smooth. Beat in the sardines, anchovy paste, lemon juice, Worcestershire sauce, and cayenne.

☐ Serve with crackers or use as a dip for vegetables.

YIELDS 1½ CUPS.

INGREDIENTS:
8 OUNCES CREAM CHEESE, SOFTENED
1 CAN SARDINES, DRAINED AND MASHED
1 TABLESPOON ANCHOVY PASTE
1 TEASPOON LEMON JUICE
1 TEASPOON WORCESTERSHIRE SAUCE
CAYENNE PEPPER TO TASTE (OPTIONAL)

Smoked Oyster Spread

☐ Mince the oysters very finely.

☐ In a bowl, beat the cream cheese and lemon juice until smooth and fluffy. Stir in the oysters and chives.

☐ Serve as a spread for crackers.

YIELDS ABOUT 1½ CUPS.

INGREDIENTS:
1 CAN SMOKED OYSTERS, DRAINED
8 OUNCES CREAM CHEESE
1 TEASPOON LEMON JUICE
2 TABLESPOONS MINCED CHIVES, SCALLIONS, OR ONIONS

Friar's Toast

INGREDIENTS:

6 SLICES OF COOKED BACON

1 CUP GRATED CHEDDAR CHEESE

¼ TEASPOON WORCESTER-SHIRE SAUCE

6 SLICES TOAST

18 PICKLED ONION SLICES

6 TABLESPOONS GRATED CHEDDAR CHEESE

☐ Preheat the broiler.

☐ Crumble the bacon into a bowl and beat in the cheese and Worcestershire sauce.

☐ Spread thickly on toast slices. Top each toast with 3 overlapping onion rings and sprinkle with grated cheese.

☐ Broil until the cheese is melted and starts to brown. Cut into squares, if desired.

YIELDS 8 TO 32 TOASTS.

Tuna Paté

INGREDIENTS:

7 OUNCES TUNA IN OIL, DRAINED

1 TABLESPOON SOFTENED BUTTER

½ CUP HEAVY CREAM

2 TABLESPOONS DRAINED CAPERS

1½ TABLESPOONS MINCED PARSLEY

1 TEASPOON GRATED LEMON RIND

1 TEASPOON LEMON JUICE

SALT AND PEPPER TO TASTE

☐ In a bowl, mash the tuna and butter until smooth.

☐ Beat the cream until it forms soft peaks and fold it into the fish with the capers, parsley, lemon rind, lemon juice, salt, and pepper.

☐ Pack into a crock and chill until ready to serve. Can be kept for 2 to 3 days. Serve with crackers.

YIELDS ABOUT 1½ CUPS.

Sardine Paté

☐ In a bowl, beat the cream cheese with the lemon juice until soft and fluffy. Beat in the onion, parsley, and sardines.

☐ Shape into a mound and sprinkle with the parsley. Serve with crackers.

YIELDS ABOUT 1 CUP.

INGREDIENTS:
½ POUND CREAM CHEESE
1 ½ TABLESPOONS LEMON JUICE
1 TABLESPOON MINCED ONION
1 TABLESPOON MINCED PARSLEY
6 OUNCES SARDINES, DRAINED AND MASHED
MINCED PARSLEY

Shellfish en Brochette

This same marinade can be used for beef, pork, lamb, chicken, or liver chunks.

☐ In a bowl, combine the oil, sherry, gingerroot, and garlic.

☐ Cut the lobster tails into chunks.

☐ Marinate the lobster, shrimp, and scallops for at least 30 minutes.

☐ When ready to cook, drain the shellfish, skewer on bamboo skewers, and brush lightly with the soy sauce.

☐ Broil, turning, until lightly browned. Do not overcook.

YIELDS 6 SKEWERS.

INGREDIENTS:
¼ CUP OLIVE OIL
¼ CUP DRY SHERRY
1 TEASPOON MINCED GINGERROOT
¼ TEASPOON CRUSHED GARLIC
3 WHOLE LOBSTER TAILS, COOKED
6 SHRIMP, COOKED AND PEELED
6 SCALLOPS, UNCOOKED
1 ½ TABLESPOONS SOY SAUCE

Swordfish Brochettes

In larger quantity, these and the other brochettes can be served as a main course.

INGREDIENTS:

1 POUND SWORDFISH
5 TABLESPOONS OLIVE OIL
1 TABLESPOON LEMON JUICE
2 TEASPOONS GRATED ONION
¼ TEASPOON PAPRIKA
SALT TO TASTE

☐ Preheat the broiler.

☐ Cut the swordfish into 1½-inch cubes and place in a bowl. Combine the remaining ingredients, mix well, and pour over fish. Let marinate for at least 1 hour.

☐ Broil about 10 to 15 minutes or until just cooked.

YIELDS ABOUT 12 SKEWERS.

Shrimp Aillade

Shrimp come packed so many to the pound. I find that 20 to 30 to the pound is suitable for this preparation. Jumbo shrimp may be impressive to look at, but they are really too big for an hors d'oeuvre — and too expensive.

INGREDIENTS:

1 POUND OF SHRIMP, COOKED
  AND PEELED
3 CLOVES GARLIC, CRUSHED
1 TABLESPOON LEMON JUICE
12 TO 14 WALNUTS, MINCED
¾ CUP OLIVE OIL
½ TEASPOON SALT
MINCED PARSLEY

☐ Devein the shrimp.

☐ In a bowl, combine the garlic, lemon juice, walnuts, and oil with the salt. Mix in the shrimp and sprinkle with parsley.

☐ Serve with wooden skewers.

YIELDS 20 TO 30 SHRIMP.

Gambas Al Ajillo

Shrimp in Garlic

☐ Peel the shrimp, leaving the tail intact. Devein.

☐ Place shrimp into a skillet and add the olive oil, garlic, parsley, and salt. Let marinate for 1 hour.

☐ Cook over high heat until shrimp are just cooked. Let guests skewer them directly from the skillet.

YIELDS 30 TO 40 SHRIMP.

INGREDIENTS:

1½ POUNDS MEDIUM SHRIMP, 20 TO 30 PER POUND

¾ CUP OLIVE OIL

3 WHOLE GARLIC CLOVES, PEELED

1 TABLESPOON MINCED PARSLEY

½ TEASPOON SALT

Barbecued Chicken Wings

If you prefer, you can prepare the marinade at home. It will keep for a week in a cool place. Use the marinade on pork, chicken, or steak, as well as on the chicken wings.

☐ In a bowl, mix together the tomato purée, molasses, vinegar, oil, mustard, garlic, Worcestershire sauce, and Tabasco.

☐ Cut off the wing tips and discard. Separate the first and second joints and arrange in a layer in a shallow dish. Pour the marinade over the chicken wings and let stand for anywhere from 30 minutes up to 3 hours, turning occasionally.

☐ Toward the end of the marinating time, preheat the broiler.

☐ Broil for about 15 minutes, basting often with the marinade. Turn and broil the other side, basting often.

YIELDS 24 PIECES.

INGREDIENTS:

⅔ CUP TOMATO PURÉE

¼ CUP MOLASSES

¼ CUP CIDER VINEGAR

2 TABLESPOONS VEGETABLE OIL

1½ TABLESPOONS DIJON MUSTARD

2 GARLIC CLOVES, MINCED

2 TEASPOONS WORCESTERSHIRE SAUCE

½ TEASPOON TABASCO SAUCE

12 CHICKEN WINGS

Sesame Chicken Brochettes

This marinade can be prepared at home. If you prefer, purée the cup of chutney in a blender or processor and bring on board ready to use.

INGREDIENTS:

1 POUND CHICKEN, SKINNED AND BONED

3 TABLESPOONS DRY WHITE WINE

1 TABLESPOON MINCED CHUTNEY

1½ TABLESPOONS OLIVE OIL

1½ TEASPOONS CURRY POWDER

¾ CUP SESAME SEEDS

½ CUP CHUTNEY

☐ Cut the chicken into 1½-inch pieces.

☐ In a bowl, combine the wine, chutney, olive oil, and curry powder.

☐ Marinate the chicken for at least 1 hour, stirring occasionally. Toward the end of the marinating time, preheat the broiler.

☐ Roll the chicken pieces in the sesame seeds and skewer.

☐ Broil until cooked through, basting with the marinade, about 10 minutes.

☐ Pick out the larger pieces of chutney and chop finely. Mix into the chutney syrup and use as a dip for the cooked chicken.

YIELDS ABOUT 12 SKEWERS.

Indonesian Chicken Sate

INGREDIENTS:

2 CHICKEN BREASTS, CUT INTO 1-INCH CUBES

¼ CUP BUTTER

¼ CUP SOY SAUCE

½ TEASPOON CRUSHED CORIANDER

2 TABLESPOONS LIME JUICE

SESAME SAUCE, SEE FACING PAGE

☐ Preheat the broiler.

☐ Skewer the chicken pieces.

☐ In a saucepan, melt the butter and stir in the soy sauce, coriander, and lime juice. Brush the chicken with the butter mixture.

☐ Broil until tender and brown, about 10 to 15 minutes, basting often with the butter mixture.

☐ Serve as an appetizer or as a main course with the sesame sauce.

YIELDS ABOUT 12 SKEWERS.

Sesame Sauce

Although this can be prepared on board, it is easier to prepare it ahead and bring it in a container. It keeps for several weeks chilled and can be used to accompany any broiled meat or as a dip for vegetables. It can be served with fish, but frankly, the sauce often overpowers the fish.

Sesame paste, sesame oil, dark soy sauce, chili paste with garlic, rice vinegar, and chili oil are all available in Oriental markets and some supermarkets. Peanut butter can be substituted for sesame paste, if desired.

☐ In a bowl, beat the sesame oil and paste until smooth. Beat in the soy sauce, chili oil, chili paste, vinegar, ginger, scallions, garlic, and coriander, if desired.

YIELDS ABOUT 1 CUP OF SAUCE.

INGREDIENTS:

2 TABLESPOONS SESAME PASTE

2 TABLESPOONS SESAME OIL

1 TABLESPOON DARK SOY SAUCE

1½ TEASPOONS CHILI OIL

1 TABLESPOON CHILI PASTE WITH GARLIC

1 TABLESPOON RICE VINEGAR

1½ TEASPOONS MINCED GINGER

1½ TEASPOONS MINCED SCALLIONS

1½ TEASPOONS MINCED GARLIC

3 TABLESPOONS MINCED CORIANDER (OPTIONAL)

Bacon-Wrapped Foods

Bacon wrapped around almost anything makes a popular hors d'oeuvre. In fact, almost any smoked meat or fish wrapped around an imaginative filling makes a very pleasing hors d'oeuvre. Chicken livers wrapped in bacon, possibly with a piece of water chestnut, are wonderful. But so are scallops, shrimp, prunes, olives, or Brazil nuts. Broil them until the bacon is crisp. Prosciutto works well wrapped around melon, strawberries, or pears and served cold. You can also wrap it around scallops, shrimp, or swordfish chunks and grill until the fish is cooked. Ham wrapped around strips of cheddar or Gruyère cheese can be served cold or grilled until the cheese is just warmed.

Roast Beef Rolls

These rolls can be filled with all sorts of goodies. Use strips of cheese or a pickle instead of the anchovy.

INGREDIENTS:
½ TEASPOON DRY MUSTARD
WATER
12 THIN SLICES OF RARE
    ROAST BEEF
ANCHOVY FILLETS
2 TABLESPOONS MINCED
    ONION
MINCED PARSLEY

☐ In a bowl, mix the mustard with enough water to make a smooth paste.

☐ Spread each slice of beef with mustard paste and lay anchovy fillets along one end of the roast beef. Sprinkle with onion and parsley. Roll tightly and cut into 1½-inch lengths.

☐ Secure each piece with a skewer and dip each end into parsley, if desired.

☐ Spread the beef with butter mixed with crushed garlic, salt, pepper, and some minced parsley, or butter mixed with crushed garlic, minced basil, salt, and pepper.

YIELDS ABOUT 36 PIECES.

Roquefort Roast Beef Rolls

Try other meats instead of the roast beef, such as thin slices of turkey, Genoa salami, or Mortadella.

☐ Force the Roquefort through a sieve into a bowl and beat in the butter and Cognac to make a smooth mixture.

☐ Spread the Roquefort butter on the roast beef slices, roll tightly, and chill for about 30 minutes. Cut into 2-inch lengths, dip the ends in the parsley, and serve.

INGREDIENTS:
4 OUNCES ROQUEFORT
4 OUNCES BUTTER
1 TEASPOON COGNAC
½ POUND ROAST BEEF, RARE
3 TABLESPOONS MINCED
PARSLEY

YIELDS ABOUT 36 PIECES.

Pakistan Kebabs

☐ In a bowl, mix together the beef, parsley, onion, garlic, gingerroot, turmeric, coriander seed, red pepper flakes, salt, and yogurt.

☐ Form into small sausages and press onto skewers.

☐ Grill, preferably over charcoal, until crusty and brown. The kebabs should be rare to medium.

INGREDIENTS:
1½ POUND LEAN GROUND
BEEF
1 TEASPOON MINCED
PARSLEY
1 LARGE ONION, GRATED
2 GARLIC CLOVES, MASHED
1 TEASPOON MINCED
GINGERROOT
½ TEASPOON TURMERIC
½ TEASPOON CORIANDER
SEED
½ TEASPOON RED PEPPER
FLAKES
SALT TO TASTE
3 TABLESPOONS YOGURT

YIELDS ABOUT 16 PIECES.

Olive-Stuffed Meatballs

INGREDIENTS:
1 POUND GROUND BEEF
½ CUP MINCED ONION
½ CUP BREAD CRUMBS
1 EGG, LIGHTLY BEATEN
½ TEASPOON SALT
½ TEASPOON PEPPER
36 PIMIENTO-STUFFED OLIVES
3 TABLESPOONS OIL

☐ In a bowl, mix together the beef, onion, bread crumbs, egg, salt, and pepper.

☐ Shape into 1-inch balls and make a hole in the center of each. Insert an olive in the hole and press the meat over it.

☐ Sauté in the oil until golden or grill over charcoal.

YIELDS ABOUT 25 MEATBALLS.

Smoked Sausage with Mustard Dressing

Any smoked sausage can be used in this recipe: smoked links, kielbasa, cervelat, or chorizo.

INGREDIENTS:
1½ POUNDS SMOKED
   SAUSAGE LINKS
1 TABLESPOON VEGETABLE
   OIL
1 TABLESPOON PREPARED
   MUSTARD
½ TEASPOON MUSTARD SEED
1 TABLESPOON WINE
   VINEGAR
½ TEASPOON SALT
½ TEASPOON PEPPER

☐ Simmer the sausages in water to cover until they are heated through. If desired, peel the skin and cut into chunks. (Performing this step at home is a good idea.) Keep sausages warm in the cooking liquid.

☐ In a bowl, beat the oil, mustard, mustard seed, vinegar, salt, and pepper together.

☐ Add the sausage, toss gently, and serve with wooden skewers.

YIELDS ABOUT 36 PIECES.

Potted Braunschweiger

Braunschweiger is smooth, creamy liverwurst. Buy a more expensive brand to get one that is smooth and soft, rather than firm. This is the quick replacement for pâté, flavorful and easy to prepare. You can prepare it at home and bring it on board in a resealable container.

☐ In a bowl, beat the braunschweiger and sour cream until well blended. In a skillet, sauté the mushrooms in the butter until they are browned and the liquid has evaporated. Add the parsley and thyme and sauté 1 minute.

☐ Beat the mushroom into the braunschweiger with the Cognac. Correct seasoning with pepper. Pack into a crock.

YIELDS ABOUT 4 CUPS.

INGREDIENTS:

1 POUND BRAUNSCHWEIGER (LIVERWURST)

½ CUP SOUR CREAM

½ POUND MINCED MUSHROOMS

3 TABLESPOONS BUTTER

2 TABLESPOONS MINCED PARSLEY

¾ TEASPOON THYME

¼ CUP COGNAC

PEPPER TO TASTE

THREE

SOUPS, STEWS, AND SANDWICHES

Recently I was asked what kind of soup to serve in the middle of a North Atlantic gale. The answer: *none.* Save soups for calmer weather. You may think that the warmth of soup would be appreciated – and it would – but rough seas invite burned hands, cursing captains, and a very messy galley, cabin, and cockpit.

Soups are delicious if the weather is cold and you have just gotten into port. There are some soups that can be prepared within a short period of time. These are worth knowing about and perhaps worth having on hand. You can of course use canned soups, but, frankly, the only advantage is that they heat up quickly. The flavor, with few exceptions, is disappointing, to say the least. If you know the weather will be cold, then freeze some soups and take them along, so you can serve real soup in the same time it would take to open and warm the contents of a can. Otherwise, prepare your own.

Ideally, you will make your own chicken stock and freeze it to bring on board. You will be so well organized that you will freeze it in containers of 1-, 4-, and 8-cup capacity so that you can defrost the proper quantity when you need it. You will have a bit of leftover chicken stock to enhance the sauce for a sautéed chicken or to boil with vegetables. Of course, most of us are not that organized and will remember only just before we pack to sail that we wanted chicken stock. Canned stock is acceptable, especially if you can find one without salt. Bouillon cubes *sometimes* work. Just take into account the large amount of salt. Do not add any salt until the dish is ready to serve. Then taste it and add salt if needed.

With chicken stock on hand, it takes just a few minutes and no real recipe to prepare a soup. Sauté some minced onions with a pinch of minced garlic until soft, in butter or olive oil. Add stock and simmer 2½ minutes. Add a selection of vegetables such as diced potatoes and carrots, simmer until almost tender, and add some fresh, finely shredded spinach, lettuce, cabbage, or romaine, with some corn or those ubiquitous leftovers. Simmer until tender and, if desired, finish with ½ cup of milk. Correct the seasoning with salt and pepper and add a favorite herb. Note: add one herb, not several.

This brings up a very important point, not only for soups, but for all cooking. Use one herb, or possibly two, to give a predominant flavor to your dish and to produce a delicious result. If you add a great variety of herbs and spices, you will produce an indistinct flavor and give the dish a sort of muddy quality. There are exceptions, of course. Tarragon, chervil, parsley, and chives work very well together. Indian curries are made from a large number of herbs and spices, but it takes considerable knowledge of these to achieve a successful flavor. Build your knowledge of seasoning conservatively. Add one or two herbs or spices, perhaps three or four, after careful consideration. With a soup, you can test your seasonings easily by taking a little soup out of the pot and adding the herbs separately, mixing, and then tasting. If it is good, return it to the pot. If not, discard.

Some of the recipes included here might just as appropriately be considered main courses and filed under "Meat," "Fish," or "Poultry" – and the distinction does, at times, become pretty academic. I use "stew" in the sense of a one-pot preparation. Others might call it a "casserole," but frankly, the term has never made much sense to me. A casserole is simply a dish or pot in which one cooks a stew.

Stews, in the sense of meat stews made from the tougher cuts of beef cooked lovingly for long periods of time, are not the stuff of this book. You are not supposed to be cooking that long. Although the stove does most of the work, you will still have to watch. Also, if it is cold enough to call for a stew like that, all too often the weather and seas are rough enough so that long simmering is not the wisest way to cook.

There are stews made of fish (freshly caught, we hope) and some chicken and meat stews that take a relatively short time to prepare. You might start the meal while preparing lunch. Brown the meat and vegetables, arrange them in their cooking pot, and assemble the cooking liquid. When you are ready to cook the meal, heat them separately, combine, and let simmer for an hour or so while you have a drink and talk with friends from other boats. If you make the stew in large quantity, you can have tomorrow's meal ready in advance, or invite some fellow sailors to join you. There is no doubt that once these flavors start to waft across the waters, you will have plenty of friends.

Fish stews are ready in about 20 minutes. Make sure that you do not overcook them. Prepare everything and start cooking very shortly before you plan to serve.

If you are planning on serving a meat or chicken stew on your voyage, save yourself some trouble by cutting the meat up before you leave. (You save space by discarding the unusable portions, and you can use the chicken bones for stock.)

Freeze the meat until you want it, but be careful that it does not thaw before you are ready to use it.

To tell people how to make sandwiches is a risky business. There are those who are convinced that a sandwich should be no less than two and a half stories tall, with no fewer than 15 ingredients, while others consider a single slice of paper-thin ham between two thin slices of lightly buttered bread to be perfect. You must take into account the people for whom you are cooking, or at least for whom you are buying provisions. There are some perfectly acceptable adults who like, if not love, peanut butter and jelly. If that is the case, let them have it. Others of us would prefer fresh French bread with goat cheese and sun-dried tomatoes drizzled with rosemary-and-garlic-flavored olive oil. We do not always get our way. We can have the goat cheese, the sun-dried tomatoes, and even the rosemary-and-garlic-flavored oil. What we cannot have on a boat is French bread. My good friend, Alice, made it very clear one day that it was not acceptable to bring a good crusty loaf of French bread onto a boat. No matter how careful you are, the crumbs fly all over the place. She explained that it does not make any difference where you try to slice it, the crumbs still go flying. She insists (correctly) that even if you lean over the side and slice the bread, the crumbs will end up back in the galley – over, under, and in everything. Unless you want to spend a lot of time cleaning the galley, avoid so-called French bread with its very crumbly crust. Another point is that the shelf life of a properly made loaf is less than 6 hours. Do not feel deprived. You can stock ordinary white bread, whole wheat, pumpernickel rye, caraway rye, Russian rye, any rye, and breads of that ilk. For emergencies, store a few packages of those foil-wrapped pumpernickels and bauernbrots from Germany that are very dense and have a shelf life of several months. I have never considered it necessary to buy canned breads. The one version I sampled tasted canned. You can make quick breads to serve with dinner, such as baking powder biscuits and muffins, but, again, you are on vacation. Let them eat pasta!

Sandwich fillings can be limited to a few items. Most people tend to have a favorite sandwich, and when you mention the word *sandwich*, that is what they want. The peanut butter and jelly guy, the cold-cuts man, the frankfurters and hamburgers set are all cases in point. Canned tuna, shrimp, or crab can be made into a quick salad spread that you can extend by adding a chopped hard-cooked egg or two. Or try an egg salad sandwich. If you moor at a port with a store that sells sliced roast beef, ham, and cheese, so much the better. A favorite combination recently has been roast beef with an herbed, peppered cheese spread. It is wonderful on French bread, but it works very well on caraway rye or light rye.

Do not store sliced roast beef for more than two days on ice. Vacuum-packed cold cuts do have a longer life, but once the package has been opened, they should be consumed within a day or two. If any of the meats should start to feel slippery or develop a white bloom, it is safer to feed them to the fish. You may lose a little money, but better that than end your cruise early.

Corn Chowder

☐ In a kettle, render the pork fat over moderate heat, stirring often, until the pork is crisp and brown. Transfer the bits to paper toweling to drain.

☐ Sweat the onions in the fat in the kettle until soft, but not brown.

☐ With a sharp knife, cut the kernels from the ears of corn and add to the kettle.

☐ Add the potatoes and water and simmer until the potatoes are tender, about 15 minutes.

☐ Add the milk and cream and cook, stirring, for 5 minutes. Season with salt and plenty of pepper. Add the reserved pork bits.

INGREDIENTS:

3 OUNCES LEAN SALT PORK, IN ¼-INCH DICE

4 MEDIUM ONIONS, THINLY SLICED

4 EARS OF CORN

3 POTATOES, IN ¼-INCH DICE

2 CUPS WATER

1 CUP MILK

1 CUP LIGHT CREAM

SALT AND PEPPER TO TASTE

YIELDS ABOUT 6 SERVINGS.

Simple Summer Borscht

☐ Drain the liquid from the beets and combine it with consommé and half of a soup can of water. Stir in the sugar and bay leaf and bring to a boil.

☐ Grate the beets and stir them into soup. Simmer 5 minutes.

☐ Correct seasoning with lemon juice, salt, pepper, and sugar, if you want to create a sweet-sour taste. Remove bay leaf.

☐ Serve hot or cold with a dollop of sour cream.

INGREDIENTS:

1 CAN (16 OUNCES) WHOLE BEETS

1 CAN (10½ OUNCES) BEEF CONSOMMÉ

1 TABLESPOON SUGAR, OR TO TASTE

1 LARGE BAY LEAF

JUICE OF 1 LARGE LEMON

SALT AND PEPPER TO TASTE

1 PINT SOUR CREAM

YIELDS ABOUT 4 SERVINGS.

Gazpacho
Cold Tomato Vegetable Soup

INGREDIENTS:

1½ CUPS CUBED WHITE BREAD, TOASTED

1 TABLESPOON SALT

1½ TEASPOONS CUMIN

3 TABLESPOONS OLIVE OIL

1 TO 4 CLOVES GARLIC, CRUSHED

3 CUPS TOMATO JUICE

3 CUPS COLD WATER

BLACK PEPPER TO TASTE

CAYENNE PEPPER TO TASTE

2 TO 4 TABLESPOONS VINEGAR (OPTIONAL)

3 ICE CUBES

1 ONION, FINELY DICED

2 GREEN PEPPERS, FINELY DICED

2 STALKS CELERY, FINELY DICED

1 CUCUMBER, FINELY DICED

3 TOMATOES, PEELED AND DICED

2 TO 3 CUPS CUBED BREAD, SAUTÉED

☐ In a bowl, combine the bread, salt, cumin, olive oil, garlic, and tomato juice; let stand for 15 minutes; then beat with a wire whisk until fairly smooth. Add the cold water and more salt, if needed.

☐ Season with black pepper, cayenne, and vinegar, and stir in the ice cubes. Chill.

☐ Serve the soup with bowls of the remaining ingredients on the side, or, if desired, stir them in just before serving.

☐ This soup means a fair amount of work with all that dicing, but it is cool and refreshing. For a short cruise, it could be prepared at home, with all the ingredients brought in separate containers.

YIELDS ABOUT 6 SERVINGS.

Cold Mustard Cream Soup

This is a truly wonderful soup to serve hot or cold. If you like, prepare it at home and bring it on board well chilled. Serve it with a sprinkle of chives, if possible.

☐ In a saucepan, melt the butter, add the flour, and cook, stirring, for 2 minutes.

☐ Remove from heat and stir in the mustard. Add the stock, light cream, salt, pepper, and onion, and bring to a boil, stirring. Simmer 10 to 15 minutes.

☐ In a bowl, combine the egg yolks and heavy cream. Add some of the hot liquid to this mixture and return to the saucepan.

☐ Cook, stirring, about 1 minute without boiling. Strain and chill.

INGREDIENTS:

2 TABLESPOONS BUTTER

2 TABLESPOONS FLOUR

3 TO 4 TABLESPOONS DIJON MUSTARD

2½ CUPS CHICKEN STOCK

1¼ CUPS LIGHT CREAM

SALT AND PEPPER TO TASTE

1 TABLESPOON MINCED ONION

2 EGG YOLKS

3 TABLESPOONS HEAVY CREAM

YIELDS ABOUT 6 SERVINGS.

Potage de Pommes de Terre aux Verdures
Potato Soup with Greens

☐ In a large kettle, combine the potatoes, onion, leek, celery, watercress, parsley, water, salt, and pepper. Simmer until the potatoes are tender.

☐ Strain and mash the potatoes. Return these to the liquid with the butter and correct the seasoning with salt and pepper. Reheat.

☐ Add cream and serve hot. This soup is also good served cold.

INGREDIENTS:

3 POTATOES, CHOPPED

1 LARGE ONION, MINCED

1 LARGE LEEK, MINCED

1 STALK CELERY, MINCED

½ CUP MINCED WATERCRESS

½ CUP MINCED PARSLEY

3 CUPS WATER

1½ TABLESPOONS BUTTER

CREAM TO TASTE

SALT AND PEPPER TO TASTE

YIELDS ABOUT 6 SERVINGS.

Soup aux Legumes

Vegetable Soup

INGREDIENTS:

4 TABLESPOONS BUTTER

2 TABLESPOONS MINCED PARSLEY

2 GARLIC CLOVES, CRUSHED

SALT AND PEPPER TO TASTE

8 TO 10 CUPS CHICKEN STOCK

2 POTATOES, CUT INTO THIN STICKS

1 CUP TURNIP, CUT INTO THIN STICKS

2 STALKS CELERY, CUT INTO THIN STICKS

2 CUPS SHREDDED CABBAGE

2 CARROTS, CUT INTO THIN STICKS

5 PEPPERCORNS

1 CUP GREEN BEANS, CUT INTO 1-INCH PIECES

1 CUP PEAS

☐ In a bowl, mash together the butter, parsley, garlic, salt, and pepper.

☐ In a kettle, simmer the stock, potatoes, turnips, celery, cabbage, carrots, salt, and peppercorns until the vegetables are very tender, about 35 minutes. Add the beans and peas and cook 15 minutes longer.

☐ Correct seasoning with salt and pepper.

☐ Serve with a dollop of the garlic butter.

YIELDS 6 SERVINGS.

Thourins

Onion Soup

INGREDIENTS:

3 TO 5 LARGE ONIONS, THINLY SLICED

2 TABLESPOONS OLIVE OIL

1 TABLESPOON FLOUR

½ CUP DRY WHITE WINE

5 CUPS HOT BEEF STOCK

6 TO 8 SLICES OF DAY-OLD RYE BREAD

½ to ⅔ CUP GRATED GRUYÈRE

☐ In a kettle, sweat the onions in the oil, covered, until very soft. Remove the cover and cook, stirring, until onions are pale golden.

☐ Stir in the flour until blended. Add the wine and stir again.

☐ Stir in the hot beef stock and cook, stirring, until it comes to a boil.

☐ In a soup tureen or individual bowls, make layers of the bread and cheese, finishing with cheese. Pour on the hot soup and let stand for a few minutes before serving.

YIELDS 4 TO 6 SERVINGS.

Potage Mentonnaise
Vegetable Soup Menton

☐ In a kettle, sweat the onions and garlic in the oil.

☐ Add the chicken stock and tomatoes and bring to a boil.

☐ Add the potatoes and beans and simmer 10 minutes. Add the zucchini and cauliflower and simmer 10 minutes longer.

☐ Add the spaghetti and simmer until tender, about 15 minutes longer.

☐ Mix the minced basil and tomato paste together and stir into the soup.

☐ Correct the seasoning with salt and pepper.

☐ Serve with Parmesan cheese on the side.

YIELDS ABOUT 8 SERVINGS.

INGREDIENTS:

2 CUPS MINCED ONIONS

2 GARLIC CLOVES, CRUSHED

3 TABLESPOONS OLIVE OIL

6 CUPS CHICKEN STOCK

2 POUNDS CANNED ITALIAN PLUM TOMATOES, DRAINED AND CHOPPED

2 CUPS DICED POTATOES

2 CUPS GREEN BEANS, CUT INTO 1-INCH PIECES

2 SMALL ZUCCHINI, DICED

1 CUP CAULIFLOWER, IN FLORETS

4 OUNCES THIN SPAGHETTI, BROKEN INTO 1-INCH PIECES

¼ CUP MINCED BASIL

1 TABLESPOON TOMATO PASTE

SALT AND PEPPER TO TASTE

GRATED PARMESAN CHEESE

Philippine Hamburger Soup

☐ Sweat the onions and garlic in the butter until soft.

☐ Add the ground meat and cook, stirring and breaking up the meat until it loses its color. Add more butter if required.

☐ Add the potatoes, tomatoes, and beef stock, correct seasoning with salt and pepper, and simmer 20 minutes or until potatoes are tender.

YIELDS 4 SERVINGS.

INGREDIENTS:

2 ONIONS, CHOPPED

1 GARLIC CLOVE, CRUSHED

2 TABLESPOONS BUTTER

1 POUND GROUND BEEF, PORK, OR LAMB

2 POTATOES, IN ½-INCH CUBES

2 TOMATOES, PEELED, SEEDED, AND CHOPPED

4 CUPS BEEF OR CHICKEN STOCK

Summer Vegetable Chowder

You may, of course, use any selection of fresh vegetables, adding more of one and less of another as desired.

INGREDIENTS:

3 LEEKS, CHOPPED

4 TABLESPOONS BUTTER

1 CUP CUT UP GREEN BEANS

1 CUP LIMA BEANS

1 LARGE TOMATO, PEELED AND SLICED

½ CUP PEELED AND DICED EGGPLANT

½ CUP DICED CARROT

½ CUP CORN KERNELS

¼ CUP RED PEPPER, CUT INTO STRIPS

¼ CUP MINCED GREEN PEPPER

¼ CUP MINCED CELERY

2½ CUPS CHICKEN STOCK

1 CUP EVAPORATED MILK

⅔ CUP WATER

2 TABLESPOONS BUTTER, MELTED

2 TABLESPOONS CORNSTARCH

½ CUP WATER

⅛ TEASPOON THYME

⅛ TEASPOON MARJORAM

SALT AND PEPPER TO TASTE

☐ In a kettle, sweat the leeks in the butter until soft. Add the green beans, lima beans, tomatoes, eggplant, carrot, corn, red pepper, green pepper, celery, and stock. Simmer for 30 minutes.

☐ Add the evaporated milk and ⅔ cup of water and simmer 10 minutes longer.

☐ In a small bowl or saucepan, combine the melted butter, cornstarch, and ½ cup water. Mix well and stir into the simmering soup.

☐ Add the thyme, marjoram, salt, and pepper and simmer 10 minutes.

YIELDS 8 SERVINGS.

Stracciatella alla Primavera
Italian Egg Drop Soup with Vegetables

☐ In a kettle, sweat the onion in the butter until soft. Add the zucchini, carrot, celery, garlic, bay leaf, basil, oregano, and rosemary. Simmer, covered, for 10 minutes.

☐ Stir in stock and romaine leaves and simmer 10 minutes.

☐ In a bowl, beat the eggs. Remove the soup from the heat and add the eggs in a slow steady stream, stirring constantly.

☐ Correct seasoning with salt and pepper.

☐ Serve with Parmesan cheese on the side.

YIELDS 8 SERVINGS.

INGREDIENTS:
3 TO 4 TABLESPOONS BUTTER
3 LARGE ONIONS, MINCED
2 SMALL ZUCCHINI, MINCED
1 CARROT, MINCED
1 CELERY STALK, MINCED
1 GARLIC CLOVE, MINCED
1 BAY LEAF
1 TABLESPOON BASIL
¾ TEASPOON OREGANO
¼ TEASPOON ROSEMARY
8 TO 10 CUPS CHICKEN STOCK
6 LEAVES ROMAINE, SHREDDED
6 EGGS
SALT AND PEPPER TO TASTE
1 CUP GRATED PARMESAN

Spinatsuppe
Norwegian Spinach Soup

☐ In a large kettle, cook spinach in boiling stock, uncovered, for 6 minutes. Pour into a sieve, reserving the stock. Press any moisture from the spinach. Chop the spinach very fine.

☐ In the kettle, melt the butter, stir in the flour, and cook for 3 minutes or until the butter is foamy and the roux starts to turn golden.

☐ Add the reserved stock, stirring over medium heat, until the soup comes to a simmer.

☐ Add the spinach and correct seasoning with salt, pepper, and nutmeg. Simmer half-covered, for 5 minutes.

☐ Serve garnished with the hard-cooked egg slices.

INGREDIENTS:
1 POUND SPINACH, CHOPPED
1 QUART CHICKEN STOCK
1½ TABLESPOONS BUTTER
1 TABLESPOON FLOUR
SALT AND PEPPER TO TASTE
PINCH OF NUTMEG
1 HARD-COOKED EGG, SLICED (OPTIONAL)

YIELDS ABOUT 4 SERVINGS.

La Soup de Poisson
Fish Soup

This is truly one of the great soups. It is wonderfully flavorful and though it requires some work, it can be made in quantity. The soup can be prepared at home and brought on board frozen. The accompanying rouille and croutons can also be made at home.

The fish trimmings listed below include the heads (with gills removed) and bodies of non-oily fish such as haddock, sole, cod, cusk, snapper, bass, etc. You can also use shrimp shells, lobster bodies and crab bodies.

INGREDIENTS:

1 CUP ONIONS, SLICED

1 CUP LEEKS, SLICED

½ CUP OLIVE OIL

6 TOMATOES, CHOPPED, OR 1 CAN (28 OUNCES) IMPORTED TOMATOES

6 CLOVES GARLIC, CRUSHED

8 SPRIGS PARSLEY

½ TEASPOON THYME

¼ TEASPOON FENNEL SEEDS

1 TEASPOON SAFFRON THREADS

½ TEASPOON DRIED ORANGE PEEL

6 TO 8 POUNDS FISH TRIMMINGS

2½ QUARTS WATER

1 TABLESPOON SALT

SALT AND PEPPER TO TASTE

ROUILLE, RECIPE FOLLOWS

CROUTONS, RECIPE FOLLOWS

GRUYÈRE CHEESE, GRATED

☐ In a large kettle, sweat the onions and leeks in the olive oil until tender.

☐ Add the tomatoes and garlic. Bring to a simmer.

☐ Add the parsley, thyme, fennel seeds, saffron, orange peel, fish trimmings, water, and salt.

☐ Boil over high heat, uncovered, for 40 minutes.

☐ Strain, pressing out the juices.

☐ Correct the seasoning with salt and pepper.

☐ Serve each guest with a bowl of soup, to which he or she adds rouille, croutons, and grated cheese, as desired.

Note: Once the broth has been strained, you can add portions of fresh fish and shellfish, if desired, and simmer until just cooked.

YIELDS 6 TO 8 SERVINGS.

Rouille

Garlic and Pepper Sauce

☐ With a large knife, mince the garlic and pimientos to a smooth paste. If possible, work in a mortar and pestle.

☐ Add the egg yolks and whisk together, adding the oil in a very slow stream until the mixture has the consistency of mayonnaise.

☐ Correct the seasoning with salt, pepper, and Tabasco sauce. It should be rather spicy.

☐ Do not freeze rouille.

YIELDS ¾ CUP.

INGREDIENTS:
4 CLOVES GARLIC
2 PIMIENTOS
2 EGG YOLKS
6 TABLESPOONS OLIVE OIL
SALT AND PEPPER TO TASTE
TABASCO TO TASTE

Croutons

☐ Rub the crust of the bread with the garlic halves.

☐ Slice the bread into ½-inch-thick slices.

☐ In a skillet, heat ¼ inch of olive oil and brown the bread slices on both sides. Drain on paper toweling.

YIELDS 6 TO 8 SERVINGS.

INGREDIENTS:
1 LOAF FRENCH BREAD
1 GARLIC CLOVE, CUT IN HALF
OLIVE OIL

Ttioro

Basque Fish Soup

INGREDIENTS:

2 CUPS CHOPPED ONION

⅔ CUP CHOPPED CELERY
WITH LEAVES

2 CLOVES GARLIC, CRUSHED

3 TABLESPOONS BUTTER

2 28-OUNCE CANS IMPORTED
TOMATOES

1 CUP CHICKEN STOCK

⅔ CUP DRY WHITE WINE

2 TEASPOONS SALT

½ TEASPOON TABASCO OR
TO TASTE

½ TEASPOON DRIED THYME

1 CUP CHOPPED PARSLEY

1 POUND FISH FILLETS, CUT
INTO 1-INCH SQUARES

☐ In a large saucepan, sweat the onion, celery, and garlic in the butter over low heat until tender, but not brown.

☐ Add the tomatoes, chicken stock, wine, salt, Tabasco, and thyme. Simmer uncovered for 30 minutes.

☐ Add the parsley and cook 2 minutes.

☐ Add the fish and simmer gently until just cooked, about 5 minutes.

YIELDS 8 SERVINGS.

Chicken and Corn Soup

INGREDIENTS:

1 CHICKEN, 2½ POUNDS,
CUT UP OR 2½ POUNDS
CHICKEN PARTS

2½ QUARTS CHICKEN STOCK

½ CUP MINCED CELERY

1¼ TEASPOONS MINCED
PARSLEY

PEPPER TO TASTE

1 TEASPOON SALT

½ POUND EGG NOODLES,
BROKEN

2 CUPS CORN KERNELS

PINCH OF CRUMBLED
SAFFRON THREADS

SALT AND PEPPER TO TASTE

☐ Simmer the chicken in the stock until just tender, about 25 minutes.

☐ Remove the chicken from the stock. Remove the meat from the bones and cut it into ½-inch pieces. Set aside.

☐ Add the celery, parsley, pepper, and salt to the stock. Bring to a full boil and add the noodles, corn, and saffron. Simmer uncovered for 10 minutes or until noodles are cooked.

☐ Return the chicken meat to the pan and reheat. Season with salt and pepper.

YIELDS 8 SERVINGS.

Maquereaux au Vin Blanc Provencale

Mackerel with White Wine

☐ Preheat the oven to 400°F.

☐ In a saucepan, sweat the onion in 1 tablespoon of oil until soft. Add the carrots, garlic, salt, pepper, vinegar, wine, cloves, bay leaf, and tomatoes. Simmer 20 minutes.

☐ In a baking dish large enough to hold the fish in one layer, spread the remaining olive oil, and season with salt and pepper. Arrange mackerel in the dish and top with 2 lemon slices. Spoon tomato sauce over fish and cover with a piece of buttered waxed paper. Bake for 15 to 20 minutes.

YIELDS 6 SERVINGS.

INGREDIENTS:
1 CUP THINLY SLICED ONION
2 TABLESPOONS OLIVE OIL
¼ CUP THINLY SLICED CARROTS
2 GARLIC CLOVES, MINCED
SALT AND PEPPER TO TASTE
2 TABLESPOONS WINE VINEGAR
2 CUPS DRY WHITE WINE
3 CLOVES
1 BAY LEAF
1 CUP PEELED TOMATOES
6 WHOLE MACKEREL
12 THIN LEMON SLICES
3 TABLESPOONS LEMON JUICE

Cabillaud Boulangère

Baked Cod with Potatoes

☐ Preheat the oven to 400°F. Butter a 9 x 13-inch baking dish. Sprinkle the dish with salt and pepper and scatter the potato slices on the bottom. Scatter the onions over the potatoes and season with salt and pepper. Dot with 5 tablespoons butter and bake, uncovered, for 15 minutes.

☐ Remove from the oven, arrange the fish on top, and dot with remaining butter. Sprinkle with the garlic, parsley, and bread crumbs. Bake 10 minutes, baste with juices in pan, and bake 10 minutes longer.

YIELDS 4 SERVINGS.

INGREDIENTS:
10 TABLESPOONS BUTTER
SALT AND PEPPER TO TASTE
1 POUND POTATOES, SLICED PAPER-THIN
½ CUP THINLY SLICED ONIONS
4 2-INCH-THICK COD STEAKS
1 GARLIC CLOVE, MINCED
3 TABLESPOONS MINCED PARSLEY
3 TABLESPOONS BREAD CRUMBS

Perches au Chablis
Fillets of Perch in Chablis

INGREDIENTS:
2 POUNDS PERCH FILLETS
4 SHALLOTS, MINCED
5 TABLESPOONS BUTTER
SALT AND PEPPER TO TASTE
1 CUP CHABLIS, HEATED
½ CUP BREAD CRUMBS
¾ CUP GRATED GRUYÈRE

□ Preheat the oven to 400°F.

□ Arrange fillets in buttered baking dish, sprinkle with shallots, and dot with butter. Season with salt and pepper.

□ Pour on the wine and bake until fish is cooked, about 10 minutes.

□ Remove from the oven, sprinkle with bread crumbs and cheese. Brown under the broiler.

YIELDS 6 SERVINGS.

Ragoût de Coquilles Saint Jacques
Scallop Stew

INGREDIENTS:
4 TABLESPOONS BUTTER
1 POUND SCALLOPS
3 TABLESPOONS COGNAC
SALT AND PEPPER TO TASTE
1 CLOVE GARLIC, MINCED
1 CUP TOMATO SAUCE
1 TABLESPOON MINCED PARSLEY
PAPRIKA TO TASTE
3 TABLESPOONS GRATED PARMESAN

□ Preheat the broiler.

□ In a skillet, melt 2 tablespoons of butter and cook scallops for 1 minute. Add Cognac and ignite. When the flames die down, season with salt and pepper.

□ Add garlic and tomato sauce. Bring to a boil and add parsley and paprika.

□ Sprinkle with cheese and brown under the broiler.

YIELDS 4 SERVINGS.

Étuvée de Coquilles Saint Jacques aux Concombres

Smothered Scallops with Cucumbers

☐ Cut each scallop crosswise into 3 thin slices, sprinkle with a few drops of lemon juice, and set aside.

☐ Cut each cucumber into 2-inch-long strips. Blanch in boiling salted water until crisp tender, about 6 minutes. Drain and set aside.

☐ In a skillet, sweat the shallot in butter until soft and and add the tomatoes, lemon juice, salt, pepper, and nutmeg. Simmer for about 12 minutes, stirring often, until thickened.

☐ Place the scallops with their juices in a large skillet, season with pepper to taste, cover, put over medium heat, shaking the pan, for 1 minute.

☐ Add the tomato mixture and the cream and cook, stirring, until slightly thickened.

☐ Add the cucumber and tarragon and reheat gently. Serve.

YIELDS 6 SERVINGS.

INGREDIENTS:

2 POUNDS SEA SCALLOPS

LEMON JUICE

1 CUCUMBER, PEELED AND SEEDED

1 TABLESPOON BUTTER

1 SHALLOT, MINCED

3 TOMATOES, PEELED, SEEDED, AND CHOPPED

JUICE OF ½ LEMON

SALT AND PEPPER TO TASTE

PINCH OF NUTMEG

½ CUP HEAVY CREAM

4 SPRIGS OF TARRAGON, MINCED

Filets de Soles aux Tomates

Sole with Tomatoes

INGREDIENTS:

1 ONION, MINCED
3 SCALLIONS, MINCED
1 GARLIC CLOVE, MINCED
4 TABLESPOONS BUTTER
2 TABLESPOONS FLOUR
1½ CUPS WHITE WINE
¾ CUP HEAVY CREAM
3 TOMATOES, PEELED, SEEDED, AND CHOPPED
1 TABLESPOON MINCED PARSLEY
PINCH OF DRY TARRAGON
1 TABLESPOON MINCED FRESH BASIL
SALT AND PEPPER TO TASTE
6 FILLETS OF SOLE
½ CUP FINE BREAD CRUMBS
¼ CUP GRATED PARMESAN CHEESE

☐ Preheat the oven to 375°F.

☐ In a saucepan, sweat the onion, scallions, and garlic in the butter until golden.

☐ Stir in the flour and cook until lightly colored.

☐ Add the wine and cook, stirring, until thickened and smooth.

☐ Stir in the cream and simmer 5 minutes. Add the tomatoes, parsley, tarragon, basil, salt, and pepper.

☐ Butter a baking dish and arrange the sole in one layer. Season with salt and pepper. Pour the hot sauce over the sole and sprinkle with bread crumbs and Parmesan.

☐ Bake for about 10 minutes or until fish is just cooked.

YIELDS 6 SERVINGS.

Teglia di Pesce al Forno

Swordfish Casserole

INGREDIENTS:

1½ POUNDS SWORDFISH
SALT AND PEPPER TO TASTE
⅔ CUP OLIVE OIL
2 POUNDS POTATOES, THINLY SLICED
1 LARGE ONION, SLICED
1 CLOVE GARLIC, MINCED
1 TABLESPOON MINCED PARSLEY
½ HOT CHILI PEPPER, MINCED

☐ Cut the swordfish into medium-thick steaks and season with salt and pepper.

☐ Brush a 2-inch-deep baking dish with oil and cover the bottom with half of the potato and onion slices. Season with salt and pepper, and arrange the fish on top in a single layer.

☐ Sprinkle with some of the oil and all of the garlic and parsley. Sprinkle with half the chili pepper.

☐ Cover the fish with the remaining potato and onion slices, season with salt and pepper, and pour on the remaining oil.

☐ Bake for about 40 minutes or until the potatoes are tender. Add the rest of the chili peppers.

YIELDS 6 SERVINGS.

Sole Gratinée à la Gasconne

Fillets of Sole au Gratin, Gascony Style

☐ Preheat oven to 350°F.

☐ Sprinkle 2 fillets of sole with chives, cover with the remaining fillets, and season with salt and pepper.

☐ Butter a baking dish and strew with the shallots and parsley. Arrange the fillets in the dish.

☐ In a saucepan, melt the butter, stir in the mustard, tomato paste, garlic, shallot, parsley, vinegar, salt, pepper, and white wine. Simmer 10 minutes and pour over the fish. Bake for 20 minutes.

☐ Carefully pour the juices from the pan into a bowl and blend in the egg yolk.

☐ Add the mushrooms and mix well. Pour over the fish, sprinkle with bread crumbs, and brown under the broiler.

YIELDS 4 SERVINGS.

INGREDIENTS:
4 FILLETS OF SOLE
SALT AND PEPPER TO TASTE
2 TABLESPOONS MINCED CHIVES
2 TABLESPOONS BUTTER
1 TABLESPOON MINCED SHALLOTS
1 TABLESPOON MINCED PARSLEY
½ TEASPOON DIJON MUSTARD
1 TABLESPOON TOMATO PASTE
1 CLOVE GARLIC, MASHED
½ TEASPOON MINCED SHALLOTS
1 TEASPOON MINCED PARSLEY
½ TEASPOON TARRAGON VINEGAR
SALT AND PEPPER TO TASTE
½ CUP DRY WHITE WINE
1 EGG YOLK
¼ POUND MUSHROOMS, SLICED AND SAUTÉED IN BUTTER
4 TABLESPOONS BREAD CRUMBS

Spezzatino di Pollo

Chicken in Tomato and White Wine Sauce

☐ In a skillet, heat the butter and oil, and brown the chicken parts until golden.

☐ Lower the heat, partially cover the pan and cook until the chicken is cooked through, about 20 minutes total. Remove from the pan and keep warm.

☐ Stir the wine into the skillet, scraping up any brown bits. Reduce by one third and add tomatoes, salt, and pepper. Simmer over moderate heat for 10 minutes.

☐ Return the chicken to the pan and simmer 10 minutes longer.

YIELDS 4 SERVINGS.

INGREDIENTS:
4 TABLESPOONS BUTTER
4 TABLESPOONS OLIVE OIL
ONE 3 TO 3½-POUND CHICKEN, CUT UP
½ CUP DRY WHITE WINE
1 POUND RIPE TOMATOES, PEELED, SEEDED, AND MINCED
SALT AND PEPPER TO TASTE

Poulet à la Nivernais

Chicken Braised in Red Wine

INGREDIENTS:

1 LARGE ONION, CHOPPED

ONE 3-POUND CHICKEN,
   CUT UP

7 TABLESPOONS BUTTER

4 CARROTS, SLICED

½ POUND EGGPLANT, DICED

2 TABLESPOONS FLOUR

1 CUP WATER

1½ CUPS RED WINE

SALT AND PEPPER

PINCH OF MARJORAM

☐ In a skillet, brown the onion and chicken in 3½ tablespoons of butter. Transfer to a casserole and set aside.

☐ Sauté the carrots and eggplant for 8 to 10 minutes. Transfer to the casserole.

☐ Melt the remaining butter in the skillet and stir in the flour. Cook, stirring, for 3 minutes. Add the water and bring to a boil.

☐ Stir in the wine, salt, pepper, and marjoram. Bring to a boil and transfer to the casserole.

☐ Simmer the casserole over low heat for 25 minutes or until the chicken is tender. (This dish may be baked in a 350°F oven for about the same amount of time.)

YIELDS 4 SERVINGS.

Chicken with Leeks and Grapes

INGREDIENTS:

ONE 3-POUND CHICKEN,
   CUT UP

3 TABLESPOONS VEGETABLE
   OIL

2 LEEKS, CUT INTO JULIENNE

2 CUPS APPLE JUICE

2 TABLESPOONS BUTTER

2 CLOVES GARLIC, MINCED

BUNCH OF PARSLEY

SALT AND PEPPER TO TASTE

½ POUND GREEN GRAPES,
   HALVED

☐ Preheat the oven to 350°F.

☐ In a skillet, sauté the chicken in the oil until browned on both sides.

☐ Add the leeks, apple juice, butter, garlic, and half the bunch of parsley, finely chopped.

☐ Season with salt and pepper, and simmer gently, covered, on top of the stove for about 25 minutes, or bake in the oven for 25 minutes.

☐ Transfer to a serving plate and garnish with grapes and the remaining parsley.

YIELDS 4 SERVINGS.

Chicken and Pork Adobo

☐ Place the chicken and pork in a 9 x 13-inch baking dish and set aside.

☐ In a bowl, combine the vinegar, water, soy sauce, peppercorns, garlic, and bay leaf. Pour over the meats.

☐ Let marinate for 1 hour, turning meats occasionally.

☐ Remove the meats from the marinade and set marinade aside. Pat meat dry with paper toweling.

☐ In a skillet, heat the vegetable oil and brown the chicken on both sides. Remove from the skillet.

☐ Brown the pork in the skillet, pour on the marinade, and cook, scraping up the browned bits, for 15 minutes.

☐ Pour into a casserole, add the chicken, and simmer, covered, until the chicken and pork are tender, about 30 minutes. (This dish may be baked in a 350°F oven for the same amount of time.)

☐ Remove the meats from the casserole and keep warm.

☐ Skim any fat from the juices and reduce the sauce to ¾ cup. Pour over the meats and sprinkle with parsley.

YIELDS 6 SERVINGS.

INGREDIENTS:

2½ POUNDS CHICKEN LEGS AND THIGHS

1½ POUNDS PORK, IN 1-INCH CUBES

¾ CUP RED WINE VINEGAR

¾ CUP WATER

¼ CUP SOY SAUCE

8 PEPPERCORNS

4 GARLIC CLOVES, CHOPPED

1 BAY LEAF

2 TABLESPOONS VEGETABLE OIL

MINCED PARSLEY

Braised Pork Chops
in Dill and Paprika Sauce

INGREDIENTS:
6 PORK CHOPS
SALT AND PEPPER TO TASTE
FLOUR
3 TABLESPOONS LARD
1½ CUPS CHOPPED ONIONS
1 GARLIC CLOVE, CRUSHED
3 TABLESPOONS PAPRIKA
1 CUP CHICKEN STOCK
⅓ CUP HEAVY CREAM
½ CUP SOUR CREAM
2 TABLESPOONS FLOUR
3 TABLESPOONS MINCED
  DILL

☐ Season chops with salt and pepper and dredge in flour. Shake off excess flour.

☐ Heat lard in skillet until very hot, add pork, and cook for 3 to 4 minutes on each side. Remove to a plate.

☐ In the skillet, sauté onions and garlic until lightly colored.

☐ Remove the skillet from the heat and stir in the paprika until the onions are well coated. Return to the heat and pour in the stock. Bring to a boil, stirring up any browned bits.

☐ Return chops to pan, cover, and simmer gently until tender, about 30 minutes. Remove meat to a platter.

☐ In a bowl, combine the heavy cream, sour cream, and flour. Pour into the skillet and cook, stirring constantly, until thick and smooth. Stir in the dill. Pour over the chops and serve.

YIELDS 6 SERVINGS.

Bermuda Onion Sandwiches

INGREDIENTS:
1 LARGE BERMUDA ONION,
  THINLY SLICED
2 TABLESPOONS SALT
1 TABLESPOON SUGAR
ICE WATER
2 TABLESPOONS MAYONNAISE,
  SEE PAGE 178
6 SLICES OF BREAD
3 TABLESPOONS BUTTER

☐ In a bowl, combine the onion, salt, and sugar with enough ice water to cover. Let stand 1 hour and drain well.

☐ Fold the onions into the mayonnaise.

☐ Butter each slice of bread and mound the onions on top.

YIELDS 6 SANDWICHES.

Pan Bagna
Stuffed French Bread Sandwich

This sandwich belongs to a group known — believe it or not — as "sat on sandwiches." They are made, wrapped, and sat upon to meld the ingredients and provide a certain warmth to bring out the flavors. To weight the sandwich, place it, well-wrapped in foil, under the seat cushions and sit on the cushion.

You can substitute Genoa salami, tuna fish, sardines, or other cold cuts for the anchovies.

□ Cut bread in half lengthwise.

□ Sprinkle both halves with the salted water and then with the oil.

□ When the bread is well impregnated, arrange the tomato slices, artichokes, mushrooms, celery, olives, and anchovies over the bottom half.

□ Cover the top and wrap the loaf in foil. Place under a weight for at least 30 minutes.

YIELDS 6 SERVINGS.

INGREDIENTS:
1 POUND LOAF FRENCH BREAD
½ CUP SALTED WATER
½ TO 1 CUP OLIVE OIL
2 TOMATOES, SLICED
4 COOKED ARTICHOKE HEARTS, SLICED
¼ CUP SLICED MUSHROOMS
1 CELERY HEART, CUT INTO STRIPS
¼ POUND BLACK OLIVES, PITTED
8 TO 10 ANCHOVY FILLETS

Egg, Anchovy, and Shrimp Sandwiches

□ In a bowl, mash the eggs, anchovy fillets, onion, and butter.

□ Fold in the mayonnaise, mustard, salt, and pepper.

□ Spread this mixture on 6 slices of bread, arrange the shrimp on top, and cover with remaining bread.

YIELDS 6 SANDWICHES.

INGREDIENTS:
3 HARD-COOKED EGGS
4 ANCHOVY FILLETS, CHOPPED
½ TEASPOON MINCED ONION
¼ CUP BUTTER, SOFTENED
1 TABLESPOON MAYONNAISE, SEE PAGE 178
1 TEASPOON DIJON MUSTARD
SALT AND PEPPER TO TASTE
½ POUND COOKED SHRIMP
12 SLICES OF BREAD

Pan Basquaise

Basque Sandwich

INGREDIENTS:

4 RED PEPPERS, PEELED AND
CUT INTO JULIENNE

4 TABLESPOONS OLIVE OIL

⅔ CUP TUNA PACKED IN
OLIVE OIL

SALT AND PEPPER TO TASTE

2 TABLESPOONS RED WINE
VINEGAR

4 TABLESPOONS MINCED
PARSLEY

3 CLOVES GARLIC, MINCED

1 LOAF FRENCH BREAD,
HALVED LENGTHWISE

4 HARD-COOKED EGGS,
SLICED

☐ In a skillet, heat the peppers in 3 tablespoons oil.

☐ Add the tuna, salt, and pepper, and cook, stirring, until the tuna flakes and is thoroughly heated.

☐ Stir in the vinegar, 2 tablespoons of the parsley, and the garlic. Simmer until the vinegar evaporates.

☐ Remove from the heat and correct seasoning with salt and pepper.

☐ Place the bread halves on a baking sheet and heat under the broiler until warm and crisp, but not brown. Top each slice with the tuna mixture and garnish with the eggs. Drizzle with the remaining tablespoon of olive oil and sprinkle with the rest of the parsley. Serve warm in sections.

YIELDS ABOUT 6 SERVINGS.

Sardine and Egg Sandwiches

INGREDIENTS:

6 SARDINES, SKINLESS AND
BONELESS

3 HARD-COOKED EGGS,
CHOPPED

3 TABLESPOONS BUTTER

1 TEASPOON GRATED
LEMON RIND

½ TEASPOON MINCED ONION

LEMON JUICE TO TASTE

SALT AND PEPPER TO TASTE

12 SLICES PUMPERNICKEL
BREAD

☐ In a bowl, mash the sardines, eggs, butter, lemon rind, and onion. Correct seasoning with lemon juice, salt, and pepper. Make sandwiches with the bread.

YIELDS 6 SERVINGS.

Minced Cold Roast Beef Sandwich

☐ In a bowl, combine the beef, onion, horseradish, salt, and pepper. Add just enough mayonnaise to bind. Use to make sandwiches.

YIELDS 6 SANDWICHES.

INGREDIENTS:

½ POUND RARE ROAST BEEF, MINCED

2 TABLESPOONS MINCED ONION

1 TABLESPOON HORSERADISH OR TO TASTE

SALT AND PEPPER TO TASTE

MAYONNAISE, SEE PAGE 178

12 SLICES BUTTERED BREAD

Beef and Potato French Bread Round

☐ Drain mushroom juice into a bowl and stir in vinegar, mustard, garlic, salt, pepper, shallots, and parsley.

☐ Thinly slice the mushrooms and add them to the dressing with the potatoes, tomatoes, and beef. Mix well.

☐ Slice the bread in half horizontally and remove the center crumb, leaving a ½-inch-thick shell. Butter generously. Fill with the meat and potato mixture and put on the top, pressing down.

☐ Wrap securely in foil and place under a weight for at least 30 minutes.

☐ Cut the loaf into wedges and serve.

YIELDS 6 SERVINGS.

INGREDIENTS:

6 OUNCES MARINATED MUSHROOMS

2 TABLESPOONS TARRAGON VINEGAR

½ TEASPOON DIJON MUSTARD

1 CLOVE GARLIC

SALT AND PEPPER TO TASTE

2 SHALLOTS, MINCED

¼ CUP MINCED PARSLEY

1 POUND SMALL POTATOES, BOILED AND SLICED

2 CUPS CHERRY TOMATOES, HALVED

1¼ POUNDS RARE ROAST BEEF OR STEAK, CUT INTO STRIPS

10-INCH ROUND LOAF FRENCH BREAD

BUTTER

Greek Country Salad Round

INGREDIENTS:
1 ROUND SESAME-SEEDED LOAF
BUTTER
1 CUCUMBER, PEELED AND SLICED
12 CHERRY TOMATOES, SLICED
6 OUNCES FETA CHEESE
4 OUNCES SALAMI, SLICED IN JULIENNE STRIPS
2 DOZEN RIPE GREEK OLIVES, PITTED
3 TABLESPOONS CAPERS
8 ANCHOVY FILLETS, DICED
4 TABLESPOONS OLIVE OIL
2 TABLESPOONS LEMON JUICE
½ TEASPOON OREGANO
SALT AND PEPPER TO TASTE
1 AVOCADO, THINLY SLICED

☐ Slice the bread in half horizontally and remove the center crumb to make shells about ½-inch thick. Butter bread generously.

☐ Place cucumber, tomato, cheese, salami, olives, capers, and anchovies in a bowl.

☐ Mix the oil, lemon juice, oregano, salt, and pepper. Pour over salad ingredients and mix well.

☐ Spoon the salad into the bread base, cover with slices of avocado, and place the cover on top. Wrap securely in foil and let stand, weighted, for at least 30 minutes.

☐ Cut into sections to serve.

YIELDS 6 SERVINGS.

Liverwurst Salad Sandwiches

INGREDIENTS:
1 POUND LIVERWURST, MASHED
½ CUP MINCED SCALLIONS
½ CUP SHREDDED LETTUCE
2 TEASPOONS DIJON MUSTARD
MAYONNAISE, SEE PAGE 178
6 SLICES WHITE BREAD
6 SLICES WHOLE WHEAT BREAD

☐ In a bowl, combine the mashed liverwurst, scallions, lettuce, and mustard. Mix well.

☐ Spread the slices of bread with mayonnaise and the liverwurst mixture.

YIELDS 6 SANDWICHES.

FOUR

FISH

Sailors do not eat fish, or at least it seems that they do not eat it as often as one might expect, perhaps because scaling and cleaning it is such a mess. Also, there are those who fish and those who sail. Those who fish tend to take their catch home. Those who sail, sail. However, there is no reason why you cannot catch an evening's meal on occasion. Forget frozen fish for a cruise. It is never as good as fresh and will probably thaw before you are ready to serve it. If you are at the source, use it. If you hate to catch fish, plan to buy it at your various ports of call when you wish to serve it.

One fish can be substituted for another in most recipes with no trouble. Sole, scrod, haddock, halibut, and flounder can all be used interchangeably. The only difference is in the time the fish takes to cook and on occasion in the way the fish is handled. Scrod tends to fall apart after it is cooked; sole usually keeps its shape. Generally, firm-fleshed fish such as swordfish or tuna can be used in some of the same preparations as whitefish, but they are usually treated with less delicacy. A delicate cream sauce would not be really appropriate, whereas a spicy tomato sauce works very well.

The real enemy in fish cookery is heat. Fish should be cooked until it is moist and tender, not dried out. It can even be slightly underdone when it is removed from the heat. The retained heat will probably be enough to finish the cooking. A bit of fish that is not fully cooked will cause no harm, and the final dish will taste much better than if it has been cooked to death.

There is the so-called Canadian rule of fish cookery, one of the few rules in cookery that does work. Cook fish 10 minutes per inch of thickness. One chef has suggested 8 minutes, considering that many people now prefer their fish less well done than in the past. I opt for 10 minutes in most instances. (Please note that the rule applies only to scale fish. Shellfish are treated differently.) A fillet of sole, cooked flat, may be done in 2½ minutes; folded over, it may take 5 minutes; if it is rolled, it may take 15 to 20 minutes. If the fish goes into a hot broth, count the cooking time from the time it enters the broth. If it starts cooking in a cold liquid, count the cooking time from the time the liquid just comes to a simmer.

Shellfish do not fit this rule. In fact, in most instances, shellfish cooks in no more than 2 to 3 minutes. For example, shucked clams, oysters, and mussels can be poached in wine stock in anywhere from 30 seconds to 1 minute. Clams and mussels steamed in their shells are ready as soon as the cooking liquid has bubbled over the top and come to a full boil, usually about 5 minutes. Occasionally you may come across a stubborn mussel that needs to simmer another minute, but usually plan on no more than 5 minutes for a full quart of mussels.

Shrimp are usually overcooked because so many food writers call for excessively long cooking times. Shrimp that are put into boiling water will be done by the time the water returns to a boil. If the shrimp are very large, under 9 to a pound, they may take a minute or two longer. If the shrimp are small, over 35 to a pound, they will be done *before* the water returns to a boil. Test shrimp as soon as their color changes to see if they are cooked. If they are almost done, give them a stir with a spoon, turn off the heat, and let the retained heat finish the cooking. This will produce tender, flavorful shrimp, not tough, dried-out pellets. If you start the shrimp in cold water, check them for doneness shortly before the water reaches a boil. They may be done. Again, if you like, let them stand in the hot liquid, off the heat, to finish the cooking. Shrimp can be cooked with the shells on or off. Serve them warm or cold with cocktail sauce, flavored mayonnaise, or drawn butter. If you are sautéing the shrimp in a sauce, add them only at the end, or else remove them as soon as they are done and finish cooking the other ingredients. Return them to the pan just to reheat.

Scallops, too, are often overcooked because recipes indicate 5 to 10 minutes or longer for cooking. In fact, scallops cook in 1 to 2 minutes. It is far better to undercook them slightly than to serve hard, overcooked scallops. Poach scallops in hot liquid until barely done. The liquid need not even boil. Depending on the size of the scallops, this may take from less than a minute to 3 minutes, but almost never longer than that. Broiling or grilling scallops on a boat is not satisfactory if you want a rich, dark brown color. There is usually not enough heat from the broiler or grill to produce such an effect, and if you try to brown them, they will overcook. If you marinate the scallops, arrange them on skewers and cook them until they are done. They will be delicious, even if they are not browned. Sautéing scallops presents the same problem. Dust the scallops lightly with flour just before putting them into very hot butter or oil, and cook them until just done. If they are an even golden brown, that is wonderful. But if they are still light in color, serve them anyway, rather than trying to get them browner and having them toughen.

Lobster, especially for those sailing the New England coast, is a treat not to be missed. There is nothing as luscious as a feast of freshly boiled lobster at the edge of the sea, or while sitting in the middle of it. Cooking lobster is simple. There are two methods, boiling or steaming. With the shortage of fuel on a boat, the best method, I think, is to steam them. Put 1 to 2 inches of water in the kettle, add the live lobsters, cover, and bring to a boil. Let them simmer for 14 to 20 minutes, depending on the size. To tell if the lobster is cooked, check the back of the lobster where the tail and the thorax meet before the lobster is cooked. The connecting membrane will be intact. When the lobster is cooked, the membrane splits and there is a distinct separation between the two sections. (For those who care, female lobsters have feathery swimmerets on the underside where the tail and body meet. The male lobster has two hard protrusions at this point.) To boil lobsters, bring to a boil enough water to cover the lobsters, add the lobsters, and cook until done. The timing is the same as for steamed lobsters. The drawbacks to boiling are the length of time it takes the water to come to a boil and the amount of fuel required to boil the water. Lobsters can also be broiled if they are split in half (while alive) – which makes for a rather messy galley, but with a hibachi, or even a regular broiler, they do not cook evenly. For boat cookery I do prefer steamed lobster. Of course, any leftover lobster can be eaten cold the next day or removed from the shell and turned into a lobster salad. You can remove the meat from the shell, reheat it in a skillet, and then prepare a simple sauce to serve as a main course. If you are doing this, remove the lobster as soon as it has heated and flavored the butter, cook the sauce, and then return the lobster to the sauce for a second reheating. Be careful not to overcook the lobster or it will become tough.

We now take a brief look at cooking methods for fish, with suggestions for the appropriate types of fish to use.

SAUTÉING

Sautéing means frying food in a small amount of fat until it is just cooked. Ideally, you use clarified butter, which burns at a higher temperature than regular butter and can be kept in a cool area without spoiling for several weeks. See page 178 for how to make clarified butter. Most fish will not stick to the pan if they are lightly coated with seasoned flour before sautéing. Seasoned flour in this case means salt, pepper, and flour, not the entire contents of the spice cabinet. You may occasionally add a particular herb such as marjoram, oregano, or thyme or a touch of a spice such as nutmeg, mace, or cayenne to change the flavor, but it is best to keep things simple.

Use fish fillets or steaks, or small whole fish. (Gently slash the sides of whole fish to prevent them from curling in the skillet.) Dust the fish lightly with seasoned flour just before cooking, being sure to shake off the excess. If you dust the flour too early, the coating will become gummy and any excess will fall into the pan and burn. In a skillet large enough to hold the fish comfortably in one layer, heat a film of butter or oil until it is quite hot, but not smoking or burning. You do not need a lot of fat. Add the fish and cook until golden on both sides. Remove the fish and serve. If desired, a quick pan sauce can be prepared by deglazing the pan with ½ to 1 cup of dry wine. Use red or white, depending on the type of fish and what you have available. Boil the wine over high heat until reduced by half, scraping up the browned bits. Enrich with a swirl of fresh butter in the hot liquid and pour over the fish immediately. If possible, sprinkle with minced parsley and add a squeeze of lemon juice.

Sautéing is suitable for all fish as well as shrimp and scallops. Shrimp do not have to be coated with flour. Shelled, cooked lobster meat can be sautéed quickly to reheat.

BROILING AND GRILLING

Broiling and grilling are almost the same thing. Strictly speaking, grilling means the heat source is below the food, such as a charcoal grill, and broiling means the heat source is above it, such as a gas or electric broiler. Whichever method you use, the principles are the same. Marinate the fish in a mixture of olive oil; vinegar, lemon juice, or lime juice; an herb, if desired; and perhaps some crushed garlic. Season with salt and pepper. Marinate for anywhere from 30 minutes to a couple of hours. When you are ready to cook, preheat the broiler or grill until very hot. Place the fish on a rack and broil until just cooked. If you are broiling a swordfish steak that is 1 inch thick, for instance, it will probably take 8 minutes to brown one side. If the center of the uncooked side is opaque except for an area about the size of a dime, then leave it alone and finish broiling the first side only. If it is larger than a quarter, turn the fish and broil it until it is just cooked. Do not worry about browning the second side. You may lose a little flavor if the fish is not browned on both sides, but better that than to have it well browned on both sides and dried out. Of course, scallops, shrimp, swordfish, and other firm-fleshed fish can be marinated, skewered alone or with vegetables, and broiled. Frankly, broiling fillets of sole or flounder is a mistake. They are too tender and delicate. If you catch your own fish, however, you can carefully score the skin and broil it whole. Let each diner remove the meat from the bones. If you try to broil thin fillets of fish such as sole, they will be cooked before they are browned, and it will be almost impossible to remove them from the broiling rack in one piece.

POACHING

Most fish are superb when poached. There are numerous recipes for poaching fish in a stock, also called a fumet or court bouillon, from which you can make a sauce. I have included a few – for those special occasions when something truly elaborate is suitable. Read the recipe carefully before you start and you will see that it describes a series of logical steps that can be followed in a reasonably relaxed manner. If you do decide to prepare one of these recipes, keep the rest of the menu simple so you do not finish cooking with the feeling that you would rather go to bed than eat dinner.

Keep the poaching liquid at the gentlest possible simmer. Once the food is simmering, cook it until it is just done. Plan on 8 to 10 minutes per inch of thickness.

Poaching is best for white-fleshed fish, shrimp, and scallops, rather than firm fish such as swordfish.

DEEP-FRYING

I do not recommend deep-frying on a boat because of the possibility for accidents. Save the deep-fried fish for serving at home. In order to deep-fry, you need a deep pot, half filled with oil at 370°F. If it spills, it can catch fire or cause serious burns. The very thought of trying to clean up the galley is appalling.

Remember that you can always substitute one fish for another. The main point is to keep to similar types of fish. If the recipe calls for swordfish, it will adapt easily to other firm, finely grained, slightly oily fish such as tuna and salmon. Replace one whitefish with another with confidence. Use scrod, halibut, haddock, flounder, or sole interchangeably. But do not forget to adjust the cooking time.

Fish with Fennel Flambé

☐ Preheat the broiler.

☐ In a bowl, combine the olive oil, fennel, thyme, parsley, wine, and anise. (Use Pernod, Ricard, Anise, or any other anise-flavored liqueur for the marinade.)

☐ Make two or three diagonal incisions on both sides of the fish so it will not curl during the cooking. Brush with the marinade.

☐ Broil the fish for 10 minutes per inch of thickness. (If you are broiling on the fantail over a hibachi, you may need to allow extra broiling time if the wind is strong.) Turn the fish once. Place the fish on a platter.

☐ In a small saucepan, warm the Cognac, ignite it, and pour it, still flaming, over the fish.

YIELDS 4 TO 6 SERVINGS.

INGREDIENTS:
½ CUP OLIVE OIL
1 TEASPOON DRIED FENNEL
1 TEASPOON THYME
2 TABLESPOONS MINCED PARSLEY
2 TABLESPOONS WHITE WINE
1 TABLESPOONS ANISE-FLAVORED LIQUEUR
1 BLUEFISH, BASS, OR PERCH, 3 POUNDS
2 TABLESPOONS COGNAC

Fish Fillets in Mustard Sauce

INGREDIENTS:

6 FISH FILLETS

1 CUP FISH STOCK OR
  BOTTLED CLAM JUICE

SALT AND PEPPER TO TASTE

2 TABLESPOONS BUTTER

1 TABLESPOON FLOUR

1 TABLESPOON DRY MUSTARD

1 CUP HEAVY CREAM

4 TO 6 TABLESPOONS DIJON
  MUSTARD

☐ Preheat the oven to 400°F.

☐ In a 9 x 13-inch baking dish, arrange the fish in one layer.

☐ Pour on the stock and season with salt and pepper.

☐ Bake, covered, for 10 minutes or until fish is just done.

☐ Pour the cooking liquid into a small pan and reduce to ¾ cup.

☐ In a saucepan over medium heat, melt the butter, stir in the flour and dry mustard, and cook, stirring, for 2 minutes. Whisk in the reduced liquid and cook until smooth and thickened.

☐ In a bowl, combine the cream and mustard and stir into the sauce. Correct seasoning with salt and pepper.

☐ Pour the hot sauce over the fish and serve. If the fish has cooled, it can be reheated in the sauce in the oven.

YIELDS 6 SERVINGS.

Bluefish with Mustard

INGREDIENTS:

2 POUNDS BLUEFISH FILLETS

3 TABLESPOONS DIJON
  MUSTARD

½ to ¾ CUP BREAD CRUMBS

OIL

SALT AND PEPPER TO TASTE

☐ Preheat broiler.

☐ Brush the fish with the mustard and sprinkle with bread crumbs and oil.

☐ Broil until browned. Turn and broil second side, taking care not to burn the crumbs.

☐ If desired, serve additional mustard with fish.

YIELDS 4 TO 6 SERVINGS.

Bass Cooked in Seaweed

☐ In a large Dutch oven, make a layer of seaweed, stuff some more seaweed into the fish, place the fish on the bed of seaweed, and cover it with the remaining seaweed. Add the water, salt, and pepper.

☐ Simmer for 10 minutes per inch of thickness.

☐ Remove the fish, skin it, and season it with salt and pepper. Serve hot or cold with melted butter or mayonnaise.

YIELDS 4 TO 6 SERVINGS.

INGREDIENTS:
ONE 3-POUND STRIPED BASS, FILLETED
2 POUNDS SEAWEED
⅔ CUP WATER
SALT AND PEPPER TO TASTE

Cabillaud Mistral
Cod with Tomatoes and Mushrooms

☐ Preheat the oven to 350°F.

☐ Cut fish into serving portions. Season with salt and pepper and dredge in the flour. Sauté over moderate heat in the oil until golden on both sides. Transfer to a baking dish.

☐ In the skillet, boil the tomatoes, mushrooms, wine, and garlic, seasoned with salt and pepper, for 20 minutes.

☐ Pour this mixture over the fish and sprinkle with the bread crumbs and melted butter. Bake 20 minutes or until crumbs are browned. Sprinkle with parsley.

YIELDS 6 SERVINGS.

INGREDIENTS:
1½ POUNDS COD STEAKS OR FILLETS
SALT AND PEPPER TO TASTE
FLOUR
3 TABLESPOONS OIL
2 TOMATOES, PEELED, SEEDED, AND CHOPPED
¾ CUP SLICED MUSHROOMS
⅓ CUP DRY WHITE WINE
1 SMALL CLOVE GARLIC, CRUSHED
½ CUP FRESH BREAD CRUMBS
3 TABLESPOONS MELTED BUTTER
MINCED PARSLEY

Tranches de Cabillaud Bretonne

Cod Steaks Brittany Style

INGREDIENTS:

4 1-INCH-THICK COD STEAKS
1 TABLESPOON LEMON JUICE
SALT AND PEPPER TO TASTE
2 TABLESPOONS BUTTER
¼ CUP WATER
¾ CUP APPLE CIDER
1 CARROT, CUT INTO
  JULIENNE
1 ONION, CUT INTO JULIENNE
2 STALKS CELERY, CUT INTO
  JULIENNE
1 TABLESPOON FLOUR
3 TABLESPOONS HEAVY CREAM
2 TEASPOONS MINCED
  PARSLEY

☐ Preheat the oven to 350°F.

☐ Sprinkle the fish with lemon juice and salt and let stand for 30 minutes. Drain off any liquid.

☐ Place fish in one tablespoon of butter in ovenproof dish. Add the water and half of the cider. Poach for 10 minutes.

☐ In a saucepan, melt ½ tablespoon butter and sweat the carrot, onion, celery, and 1 tablespoon of cider until tender. Season with salt and pepper.

☐ Drain fish, reserving liquid, and remove centerbone and skin. Arrange on a hot platter, set aside.

☐ Strain liquid into a saucepan and add remaining cider. Reduce for 3 minutes over high heat.

☐ Meanwhile, mash the remaining butter with the flour and whisk into the simmering sauce until thickened and smooth. Add the cream and parsley. Correct seasoning with salt and pepper. Scatter vegetables over the fish and pour the sauce over all.

YIELDS 4 SERVINGS.

Cabillaud à la Basquaise I
Cod Basque Style I

☐ In a skillet, heat 3 tablespoons of oil and sauté the onions over low heat until golden, stirring often.

☐ Add 1 quart of cold water, salt, pepper, allspice, and bay leaf. Simmer 15 minutes.

☐ Carefully place the fish slices on top of the first mixture and simmer 10 minutes per inch of thickness.

☐ Meanwhile, in a separate skillet, heat the remaining oil and brown bread slices on both sides.

☐ Place fish on serving plates, top with a bread slice, and pour the sauce over the top.

INGREDIENTS:
5 TABLESPOONS OLIVE OIL
4 ONIONS, MINCED
1 QUART WATER
SALT AND PEPPER TO TASTE
PINCH OF ALLSPICE
1 BAY LEAF
1½ POUNDS COD FILLETS
6 SLICES OF BREAD

YIELDS 6 SERVINGS.

Cabillaud à la Basquaise II
Cod Basque Style II

☐ Cut the cod into serving-size pieces, sprinkle with lemon juice, and let stand for 20 minutes.

☐ In a skillet, heat the olive oil until it is very hot. Dust the cod pieces with flour and sauté them in the hot oil until they are golden on both sides. They should be cooked through. If necessary, lower the heat and cook another minute. Arrange on a serving platter and keep warm.

☐ Add the tomatoes to the oil, with garlic, salt, and pepper. Reduce to a sauce. Spoon over the cod and sprinkle with parsley. Garnish with lemon wedges.

INGREDIENTS:
2 POUNDS COD FILLETS
LEMON JUICE
¾ CUP OLIVE OIL
FLOUR
3 POUNDS TOMATOES, PEELED, SEEDED, AND CHOPPED
1 TEASPOON MINCED GARLIC
SALT AND PEPPER TO TASTE
2 TABLESPOONS MINCED PARSLEY
LEMON WEDGES

YIELDS 4 TO 6 SERVINGS.

Tranches de Cabillaud à la Dijonnaise
Cod Dijon Style

INGREDIENTS:

6 SMALL COD STEAKS

SALT AND PEPPER

JUICE OF 1 LEMON

1 TABLESPOON DIJON
  MUSTARD

1½ CUPS HEAVY CREAM

5 TABLESPOONS BUTTER

½ POUND THINLY SLICED
  MUSHROOM CAPS

FLOUR

1 TABLESPOON OLIVE OIL

2 LARGE SHALLOTS, MINCED

½ CUP DRY WHITE WINE

1 TABLESPOON BEURRE
  MANIÉ, SEE PAGE 177

2 TABLESPOONS MINCED
  PARSLEY

☐ Season fish with salt and pepper and sprinkle with lemon juice. Let stand for an hour or two.

☐ In a small bowl, mix the mustard with ½ cup heavy cream and mix well.

☐ In a skillet, sauté the mushrooms in 2 tablespoons of butter over high heat until browned. Set aside.

☐ Dredge the fish in flour and sauté it in the skillet with the remaining butter and the olive oil until golden. Remove from the pan.

☐ Stir in the shallots and cook until soft. Add the wine and reduce over high heat, scraping up any browned bits, to 1 tablespoon.

☐ Add the remaining cup of cream and reduce by one third.

☐ Stir in beurre manié bit by bit until lightly thickened and smooth. You may not need all of the beurre manié.

☐ Add the mushrooms, season with salt and pepper, and heat through.

☐ Stir in the mustard-cream mixture and whisk until smooth. Do not boil. Correct seasoning with salt and pepper. Spoon over fish and garnish with parsley.

YIELDS 6 SERVINGS.

Filets de Maquereaux Mireille
Mackerel with Tomatoes and Mushrooms

☐ Season the fish with salt and pepper and dredge in the flour. Heat ¼ cup oil in a skillet and brown the mackerel on both sides. Remove to a platter.

☐ Add 2 tablespoons of oil to the skillet and sauté the mushrooms, shallot, onion, and garlic until soft. Pour over the fish.

☐ Add the tomatoes to the skillet and season with salt and pepper. Heat until warmed through. Pour around the fish. Garnish with minced parsley.

YIELDS 6 SERVINGS.

INGREDIENTS:
6 MACKEREL FILLETS
SALT AND PEPPER TO TASTE
FLOUR FOR DREDGING
¼ CUP PLUS 2 TABLESPOONS OLIVE OIL
1 CUP SLICED MUSHROOMS
1 SHALLOT, MINCED
1 TABLESPOON MINCED ONION
1 CLOVE GARLIC, MINCED
6 SMALL TOMATOES, PEELED, SEEDED, AND CHOPPED
MINCED PARSLEY

Brochettes de Saumon
Salmon on Skewers

☐ In a skillet, sauté the mushrooms in 1 tablespoon of butter until half-cooked. Let cool.

☐ Skewer the salmon and mushrooms and sprinkle with salt and pepper.

☐ Brush with butter and roll in bread crumbs, pressing them into the salmon. Grill, basting with butter, for about 15 minutes, turning often.

☐ Serve garnished with parsley and lemon. Serve additional melted butter as a sauce.

YIELDS 6 SERVINGS.

INGREDIENTS:
½ TO ¾ CUP MELTED BUTTER
18 LARGE MUSHROOM CAPS
3 POUNDS SALMON, IN 1½-INCH CUBES
SALT AND PEPPER TO TASTE
1½ CUPS BREAD CRUMBS
PARSLEY SPRIGS
LEMON WEDGES

Saumon Grillé

Grilled Salmon

INGREDIENTS:
6 SALMON STEAKS
SALT AND PEPPER TO TASTE
FLOUR
VEGETABLE OIL

□ Preheat the broiler.

□ Season the salmon with salt and pepper and roll it first in flour and then in the vegetable oil.

□ Broil about 10 minutes per inch of thickness, basting occasionally with more oil if desired.

□ The flour-oil combination helps to brown the steaks, but they can be broiled without the coating.

YIELDS 6 SERVINGS.

Salmon Steaks with Madeira Sauce

INGREDIENTS:
6 SALMON STEAKS
SEASONED FLOUR, SEE PAGE 53
¼ CUP BUTTER
18 SMALL MUSHROOM CAPS
SALT AND PEPPER TO TASTE
¼ CUP MADEIRA
1 CUP HEAVY CREAM
1 TABLESPOON BEURRE MANIÉ, SEE PAGE 177

□ Dredge the salmon steaks in flour. In a skillet, sauté the steaks in the butter until golden on both sides and cooked through. Arrange on a platter.

□ Sauté the mushrooms in the fat in the pan until tender. Pile the caps on top of each steak.

□ Stir the Madeira into the pan and reduce to 2 tablespoons, scraping up any browned bits.

□ Stir in the cream and reduce by half. Correct seasoning with salt and pepper. Whisk in enough Beurre manié to thicken the sauce. Pour over the steaks.

YIELDS 6 SERVINGS.

Moules Marinières
Steamed Mussels

☐ Scrub mussels well and pull off beards.

☐ Put the mussels in a large kettle with shallots, wine, 1 tablespoon of the butter, and the parsley sprigs. Season well with pepper.

☐ Cover and cook over high heat until shells open. Shake pot once or twice during the cooking. Remove mussels to a serving bowl and cover.

☐ Strain liquid through a very fine sieve. Return to a clean pot and reduce by half. Stir in butter and parsley. Pour over mussels and serve.

INGREDIENTS:
2½ POUNDS MUSSELS
2 TABLESPOONS MINCED SHALLOTS
1 CUP DRY WHITE WINE
3 TABLESPOONS BUTTER
2 PARSLEY SPRIGS
PEPPER TO TASTE
2 TABLESPOONS MINCED PARSLEY

YIELDS ABOUT 2 SERVINGS.

Coquilles Saint Jacques à la Moutarde
Scallops in Mustard Sauce

☐ In a skillet, sweat the shallots in the butter until soft. Add the vinegar and simmer until almost evaporated. Add the cream and reduce by half. Add the scallops and season with salt. Cook, shaking the skillet, for about 1 minute.

☐ Remove the skillet from the heat and swirl in the mustard. If necessary, put the skillet back over the heat to finish cooking. However, the scallops should be done enough at this point. Sprinkle with parsley and serve.

INGREDIENTS:
1 TABLESPOON MINCED SHALLOTS
1 TABLESPOON BUTTER
2 TABLESPOONS RED WINE VINEGAR
1 CUP HEAVY CREAM
1 POUND SCALLOPS
SALT TO TASTE
1 TABLESPOON DIJON MUSTARD
1 TABLESPOON MINCED PARSLEY

YIELDS 4 SERVINGS.

Scallops in Cognac

INGREDIENTS:
¼ POUND BUTTER
1 CUP COGNAC
½ CUP LEMON JUICE
1 TEASPOON SALT
2 TABLESPOONS MINCED
 GINGER
¼ CUP MINCED PARSLEY
2 POUNDS SCALLOPS

☐ In a large skillet, melt the butter and add the cognac, lemon juice, salt, ginger, and parsley. Simmer 5 minutes.

☐ Add the scallops and cook, stirring once or twice, until just cooked, about 3 minutes.

☐ Remove scallops to warm serving bowl. Boil sauce over high heat until reduced by half. Pour over scallops.

YIELDS 6 SERVINGS.

Vieiras de Santiago
Scallops Spanish Style

INGREDIENTS:
¼ CUP MINCED ONION
2 GARLIC CLOVES, MINCED
2 TABLESPOONS OLIVE OIL
1 POUND SCALLOPS, HALVED
2 TABLESPOONS MINCED
 PARSLEY
½ TEASPOON DRIED THYME,
 CRUMBLED
1 HOT CHILI PEPPER, MINCED
SALT AND PEPPER TO TASTE
2 CUPS SLICED MUSHROOMS
2 TABLESPOONS COGNAC
¾ CUP DRY WHITE WINE
½ CUP TOMATO SAUCE
BREAD CRUMBS
BUTTER

☐ Preheat the oven to 450°F.

☐ In a skillet, sweat the onion and garlic in the oil until soft.

☐ Add the scallops, parsley, thyme, chili pepper, salt, and pepper. Stir in the mushrooms and cook 5 minutes.

☐ Add the Cognac and ignite, shaking pan gently.

☐ Transfer the scallops and mushrooms to a shallow baking dish.

☐ Add the wine and tomato sauce to the skillet and reduce by half. Pour this mixture over the scallops and sprinkle with bread crumbs. Dot with butter and bake until golden.

YIELDS 2 TO 4 SERVINGS.

Coquilles Saint Jacques Pont de l'Isere
Bay Scallops with Tomatoes and Oil

☐ In a small saucepan, simmer ¼ cup oil, the shallots, tomatoes, and vinegar for 2 minutes.

☐ Season the scallops with salt and pepper.

☐ In a skillet, heat the remaining oil and cook the scallops, turning often, until just cooked, about 2 minutes.

☐ Spoon into serving dishes, coat with tomato sauce and sprinkle with parsley.

YIELDS 4 TO 6 SERVINGS.

INGREDIENTS:
SALT AND PEPPER TO TASTE
¼ CUP PLUS 1 ½ TABLE-
  SPOONS OLIVE OIL
¼ CUP MINCED SHALLOTS
¾ CUP TOMATOES, PEELED,
  SEEDED, AND CHOPPED
1 TABLESPOON WHITE WINE
  VINEGAR
1 ½ POUNDS SCALLOPS
2 TABLESPOONS MINCED
  PARSLEY

Coquilles Saint Jacques à l'Antiboise
Scallops Antiboise

☐ Halve tomatoes lengthwise, sprinkle with salt, and let drain on a plate.

☐ Dry scallops on paper towels and season with salt and pepper. Dredge scallops in flour and shake off excess. In a large skillet, heat the butter and sauté the scallops until lightly browned. Remove from skillet and set aside.

☐ Add mushroom slices and cook over high heat until browned. Add shallots, garlic, and tomatoes. Cook until tomatoes are heated through.

☐ Return scallops to pan and sprinkle with parsley and black pepper. Heat through.

YIELDS 6 SERVINGS.

INGREDIENTS:
6 PLUM TOMATOES, PEELED
  AND SEEDED
SALT AND PEPPER TO TASTE
1 ½ POUND SCALLOPS
FLOUR
½ CUP CLARIFIED BUTTER,
  SEE PAGE 178
BLACK PEPPER
8 SMALL MUSHROOMS,
  THINLY SLICED
2 TABLESPOONS MINCED
  SHALLOTS
1 TEASPOON MINCED GARLIC
2 TABLESPOONS MINCED
  PARSLEY

Scallops with Ginger

INGREDIENTS:
8 TABLESPOONS BUTTER
2 TABLESPOONS MINCED
  SHALLOTS
1 CARROT, CUT INTO
  ¼-INCH STICKS
1 ZUCCHINI, CUT INTO
  ¼-INCH STICKS
1 LEEK, CUT INTO SHREDS
2 TABLESPOONS MINCED
  GINGER
½ CUP DRY WHITE WINE
½ CUP HEAVY CREAM
SALT AND PEPPER TO TASTE
1½ POUNDS SCALLOPS

☐ In a skillet, heat 2 tablespoons of the butter and cook shallots, stirring, for 30 seconds. Add the carrots, zucchini, and leek and cook 30 seconds longer.

☐ Add the ginger and wine and reduce almost completely. Add the cream and reduce by half. Season with salt and pepper.

☐ Add the scallops and simmer 1 minute. Swirl in the remaining butter and serve.

YIELDS 4 SERVINGS.

Filets de Soles Murat
Fillets of Sole with Artichokes and Potatoes

INGREDIENTS:
6 FILLETS OF SOLE
MILK
FLOUR
SALT
9 TABLESPOONS CLARIFIED
  BUTTER
1 CUP POTATOES, CUT INTO
  THIN STICKS
6 TO 8 ARTICHOKE BOTTOMS,
  COOKED AND DICED
2 TABLESPOONS FRESH
  BUTTER
LEMON JUICE
PARSLEY

☐ Cut the sole into strips the size of your little finger. Dip the strips in the milk, then in the flour seasoned with salt.

☐ Heat 3 tablespoons of the clarified butter in a skillet and sauté the sole until golden, turning as required. Remove to a serving platter.

☐ In 3 tablespoons of clarified butter, sauté the potatoes over high heat until they are well browned and tender. Remove to the platter.

☐ Toss the artichokes in the remaining clarified butter until lightly browned. Arrange the artichokes on the platter.

☐ Add the fresh butter to the skillet and cook until it is hazelnut brown, squeeze in the lemon juice, and sprinkle with parsley. Pour over the fish.

YIELDS 6 SERVINGS.

Filets de Soles Gavarni
Filets of Sole with Peppers and Mushrooms

☐ In a small skillet, sauté the peppers in the olive oil until tender.

☐ In another skillet, sauté the mushrooms in the 4 tablespoons of fresh butter until tender and season with salt and garlic.

☐ Dredge the sole in the flour and cook in clarified butter until golden.

☐ Arrange the mushrooms in the bottom of a platter, cover with the fish, and garnish with the peppers.

YIELDS 6 SERVINGS.

INGREDIENTS:

3 RED PEPPERS, CUT INTO JULIENNE

3 GREEN PEPPERS, CUT INTO JULIENNE

2 TABLESPOONS OLIVE OIL

1 POUND MUSHROOMS, SLICED

4 TABLESPOONS FRESH BUTTER

SALT TO TASTE

PINCH OF CRUSHED GARLIC

6·FILLETS OF SOLE

FLOUR

6 TABLESPOONS CLARIFIED BUTTER, SEE PAGE 178

Filets de Soles aux Noix
Fillets of Sole with Walnuts

☐ Place the flour in a pie plate. In another dish, combine the eggs and cream, and in a third, mix the bread crumbs and walnuts.

☐ Dip the fillets into the flour, then the egg, and finally the bread crumbs. Let them stand on a wire rack for up to an hour before cooking.

☐ Sauté in clarified butter until golden on both sides, using just enough butter to prevent the fish from sticking. Cook over high heat so that the fish does not overcook. Remove to a serving plate, season with salt and pepper, and serve with lemon wedges.

YIELDS 6 SERVINGS.

INGREDIENTS:

FLOUR

2 EGGS

2 TABLESPOONS CREAM

1 CUP BREAD CRUMBS

½ CUP WALNUTS, FINELY CHOPPED

6 FILLETS OF SOLE

CLARIFIED BUTTER, SEE PAGE 178

SALT AND PEPPER TO TASTE

LEMON WEDGES

Delices de Soles Lucas Carton
Fillets of Sole with Tomatoes and Mushrooms

If the fish are large, fold them in half or roll them. Figure the cooking time on 10 minutes per inch of thickness. If you are making this at home, or if you are up to it, glaze the sole under the broiler before serving.

INGREDIENTS:
6 FILLETS OF SOLE
1 SMALL ONION, MINCED
SPRIG OF PARSLEY
½ CUP BUTTER
1 CUP DRY WHITE WINE
½ CUP WATER
SALT AND PEPPER TO TASTE
3 TOMATOES, PEELED, SEEDED, AND CHOPPED
4 MUSHROOMS, SLIVERED
½ CUP HEAVY CREAM

☐ Have the fishmonger save the bones from filleting the sole. In a kettle, simmer the bones with the onion, parsley, and 2 tablespoons of the butter for 6 minutes. Add the wine and ½ cup water and simmer 12 minutes. Strain and discard any scum.

☐ Butter an ovenproof dish and arrange the sole in it. Season with salt and pepper.

☐ Strew the tomatoes and mushrooms over the fish and pour in the fish stock. Cover with buttered paper and simmer for 7 to 8 minutes or until just cooked.

☐ Pour off the liquid. Stir in the cream and reduce over high heat until it reaches the consistency of a sauce. Remove from heat and whisk in remaining butter. Pour the sauce over the fish.

YIELDS 6 SERVINGS.

Fish on Skewers

Use any or all of the fish recommended, as well as shrimp and scallops.

INGREDIENTS:
¾ CUP OIL
½ CUP LEMON JUICE
1 BAY LEAF, CRUMBLED
2 TEASPOONS MINCED DILL
4 DROPS TABASCO SAUCE
2 POUNDS SWORDFISH, HALIBUT OR SALMON, CUT INTO 1-INCH CUBES
2 CUCUMBERS, CUT 1 INCH THICK
18 STUFFED GREEN OLIVES

☐ Preheat the broiler. In a bowl, combine the oil, lemon juice, bay leaf, dill, and Tabasco. Add the fish and toss to coat. Marinate for 30 minutes.

☐ Thread the fish on 12-inch skewers, alternating the cucumbers and olives.

☐ Grill until fish is just cooked, basting with the marinade. Serve immediately.

YIELDS 6 SERVINGS.

Fish with Oregano

☐ Preheat the broiler.

☐ In a bowl, mix the lemon juice, salt, and oregano. Gradually whisk in the oil and season with black pepper. Set aside.

☐ Broil fish about 2½ minutes on each side, until just cooked.

☐ Rewhisk the sauce if necessary and spoon it over the fish.

YIELDS 4 SERVINGS.

INGREDIENTS:
JUICE OF ½ LEMON
1 TEASPOON DRIED OREGANO
¼ CUP OLIVE OIL
SALT AND PEPPER TO TASTE
2 POUNDS SWORDFISH, SALMON, OR TILEFISH, CUT INTO ½-INCH STEAKS

Poached Snapper Provençale

Of course, any whitefish — such as sea bass, sole, flounder, or cod — can be substituted for the snapper.

☐ Preheat the oven to 400°F.

☐ Place the fish in a baking dish, season with salt and pepper, and pour on the wine.

☐ Bake, covered, for 10 minutes or until just done. Transfer fish to platter. Reduce liquid to 1 cup.

☐ Melt the butter in a skillet and sauté the onion until soft. Stir in the garlic and cook until light golden. Stir in the poaching liquor, tomato sauce, parsley, oregano, thyme, and rosemary. Bring to a full boil, stirring.

☐ Lower the heat, remix the cornstarch mixture, and stir it into the sauce. Correct seasoning with salt and pepper.

☐ Pour the sauce over the fish and garnish with olives and parsley.

YIELDS 6 SERVINGS.

INGREDIENTS:
6 RED SNAPPER FILLETS
SALT AND PEPPER TO TASTE
1 CUP RED WINE
2 TABLESPOONS BUTTER
¼ CUP MINCED ONION
2 GARLIC CLOVES, MINCED
3 TABLESPOONS TOMATO SAUCE
2 TABLESPOONS MINCED PARSLEY
¼ TEASPOON OREGANO
¼ TEASPOON THYME
¼ TEASPOON ROSEMARY
¼ TEASPOON CORNSTARCH, DISSOLVED IN 1 TABLE-SPOON COLD WATER
BLACK OLIVES
MINCED PARSLEY

Red Snapper with Mushrooms and Oranges

INGREDIENTS:

⅓ CUP OLIVE OIL
6 FILLETS OF SNAPPER
SALT AND PEPPER TO TASTE
FLOUR
2 CUPS SLICED MUSHROOMS
⅓ CUP DRY WHITE WINE
⅓ CUP LEMON JUICE
6 TABLESPOONS BUTTER
2 ORANGES, CUT INTO
   SECTIONS
2 TABLESPOONS MINCED
   PARSLEY
LEMON WEDGES

☐ Preheat the oven to 350°F.

☐ In a large, shallow ovenproof pan, heat the oil.

☐ Season the fish with salt and pepper and dredge in the flour. Arrange it skin side down and sauté 3 minutes. Turn the fish carefully and surround it with mushrooms.

☐ Set the pan in the oven and bake for 4 minutes. Carefully drain off the oil, leaving the fish and mushrooms in the pan.

☐ Pour on the wine, lemon juice, and butter, and bake the fish for 3 more minutes, basting often.

☐ Scatter orange sections over the top of the fish and season with minced parsley. Garnish with lemon wedges.

YIELDS 6 SERVINGS.

Shrimp with Sherry Tomato Sauce

INGREDIENTS:

2 TABLESPOONS BUTTER
⅓ CUP MINCED ONION
2 GARLIC CLOVES, MINCED
¼ TEASPOON DRIED BASIL
½ TEASPOON BLACK PEPPER
1 POUND SHRIMP, SHELLED,
   DEVEINED, AND BUTTER-
   FLIED
½ CUP CREAM SHERRY
½ CUP CHOPPED FRESH
   TOMATOES
2 TABLESPOONS MINCED
   PARSLEY

☐ In a skillet, melt the butter and sauté the onion and garlic until soft but not brown.

☐ Add the basil, pepper, and shrimp. Sauté 1 minute. Stir in sherry and tomatoes. Heat for 1 to 2 minutes longer or until the shrimp are just cooked. Sprinkle with parsley.

YIELDS 3 TO 4 SERVINGS.

Crevettes Belle Aurore
Shrimp with Tomato Cream Sauce

☐ In a saucepan, heat 1 tablespoon of the butter and cook the carrot, onion, celery, and 1 tablespoon of the shallots for 2 minutes. Sprinkle in the flour and cook until it just starts to turn golden. Stir in the wine and tomato paste. Bring to a boil, stirring.

☐ Add the milk, salt, and pepper. Cook, stirring, until all is thickened and smooth. Simmer for 10 minutes.

☐ Stir in the cream and Tabasco and simmer for 20 minutes.

☐ In a skillet, heat the remaining tablespoon of butter with remaining shallots. Add the shrimp, season with salt and pepper, and cook until the shrimp are just pink. Add the Cognac and ignite. Mix into the sauce.

☐ Serve with rice, if desired.

YIELDS 6 SERVINGS.

INGREDIENTS:
2 TABLESPOONS BUTTER
2 TABLESPOONS MINCED CARROT
2 TABLESPOONS MINCED ONION
2 TABLESPOONS MINCED CELERY
2 TABLESPOONS MINCED SHALLOTS
1 TABLESPOON FLOUR
½ CUP DRY WHITE WINE
2 TABLESPOONS TOMATO PASTE
1 CUP MILK
SALT AND PEPPER TO TASTE
1 CUP HEAVY CREAM
TABASCO SAUCE TO TASTE
¾ CUP SHRIMP, PEELED AND DEVEINED
2 TABLESPOONS COGNAC

Shrimp with Scotch

☐ Pour enough olive oil in a large skillet to cover the bottom with a thin film. Add the shallots and cook until soft. Add the shrimp, season with salt and pepper, and raise heat to high. Cook 1 minute, add wine, and simmer 1 minute.

☐ Add the whiskey and ignite. When the flames subside, serve in soup plates with noodles or rice.

YIELDS 6 SERVINGS.

INGREDIENTS:
OLIVE OIL
5 SHALLOTS, MINCED
2 POUNDS MEDIUM SHRIMP
SALT AND PEPPER TO TASTE
1 CUP DRY WHITE WINE
2 OUNCES SCOTCH WHISKEY

Espadon Mirabeau

Swordfish with Anchovies

INGREDIENTS:

¼ CAN ANCHOVY FILLETS
¼ CUP OLIVE OIL
1 POUND SWORDFISH STEAKS
BLACK PEPPER TO TASTE
½ CUP STUFFED GREEN
  OLIVES, THINLY SLICED
¼ CUP MINCED PARSLEY

☐ In a bowl, mash 2 anchovy fillets with olive oil

☐ Season fish with pepper and brush with marinade. Broil over a hot fire for about 10 minutes, brushing with marinade again. Remove to a platter.

☐ Crisscross the anchovy fillets on top of the fish and decorate the spaces between the fillets. Sprinkle parsley around the edges.

YIELDS 4 SERVINGS.

Swordfish Grilled with Cucumber Sauce

This sauce is very good with other fish, especially salmon. It can be used as a dip with crackers or raw vegetables.

INGREDIENTS:

1 CUP PEELED, SEEDED, AND
  DICED CUCUMBER
1 PINT SOUR CREAM
1 TABLESPOON WHITE WINE
  VINEGAR
1 TEASPOON SALT
PINCH OF CAYENNE PEPPER
2 TEASPOONS GRATED ONION
3 POUNDS OF SWORDFISH,
  CUT 1 INCH THICK
3 TABLESPOONS MINCED
  DILL
6 TABLESPOONS SOFTENED
  BUTTER
SALT AND PEPPER TO TASTE

☐ Preheat the broiler.

☐ In a bowl, combine the cucumbers, sour cream, vinegar, salt, cayenne, and onion. Mix well and fold in the dill. Set aside.

☐ Brush the fish with butter and broil for 3 minutes. Turn, brush again, and broil 3 minutes longer. If this side is well browned, turn and broil the other side, basting with the remaining butter until just cooked.

☐ Serve with cucumber sauce.

YIELDS 6 SERVINGS.

FIVE

POULTRY

The versatility of chicken makes it a pleasure to use. You can prepare it in hundreds of ways and it is always wonderful. Chicken is cooked whole, cut up, boned, or even ground. It is eaten hot, cold, or at room temperature.

For sailors, chicken is a delight and a problem. If refrigeration is not the best, it should be eaten within a day of boarding. With good refrigeration, it can of. course be kept longer. If you freeze it solid before bringing it on board, you can keep it several days in the ice chest, but be prepared to cook it as soon as it is almost thawed.

When you prepare your menus, consider how you are going to cook the chicken. If it is to be roasted or braised, you may want to leave it whole. If you are going to sauté or broil it, then you will want to cut it up properly (see below). It is easier to cut it up and freeze it at home. When you cut up the chicken, you can save the parts that would otherwise be discarded and use them to make a stock, which you can also freeze for soups or to finish a sauce. If you are going to serve the chicken whole, remove it from its market wrappings, remove the package of giblets and neck, and use these to make stock. Freeze the liver separately to use for pâté or to serve sautéed or broiled on a skewer. Freeze the whole chicken wrapped in freezer paper. This way the chicken will thaw evenly and there will be less chance of bacteria developing. If you are going to be sailing for an extended period, buy fresh chickens en route and serve them soon after you buy them.

Chickens are often mislabeled in markets. Rather than buy by name, such as "broiler" or "fryer," buy by weight. A broiler should weigh between 1½ to 2½ pounds. If it is larger, it will not cook through evenly and there is a good chance that the outside will be burned before the center is fully cooked. Fryers should weigh between 2½ to 3½ pounds and are cut up for frying. Chickens three pounds or larger can be roasted whole, poached, or braised.

TO CUT UP A CHICKEN

Basically there are two ways to cut up a chicken – from the back or from the front. I prefer to start from the back. Another method of cutting up a chicken is the one used by your market. The chicken is run through a saw, with the objectionable consequence that there are splinters of bone in the meat. When *you* cut the chicken, you will have one bone in each piece. The chicken will also be easier to eat and it will lie flat in the pan to cook more evenly.

Remove the innards from the chicken, pull off any clumps of fat in the tail opening, and stand the chicken on its "knees" with the back toward you. With a large sharp knife, starting at one side of the neck opening, cut straight down in a single movement along the side of the backbone. Again, with the knife, starting at the other side of the neck, cut down with a single firm stroke. Save the backbone for stock. (You may have some trouble cutting through the hip joint, but be firm.) Open the chicken like a book and place one hand under the breastbone. With the other hand on the opened neck area, spread the chicken open and push up under the breastbone until it pops up. Sometimes this is very easy, sometimes you have to work at it, but it will come up. Run your fingers down either side of the breastbone (on the inside of the chicken) under the membrane and remove the breastbone. Set it aside with the backbone. In a young chicken, the breastbone will come out in two sections; one a sort of liver color and the other an opaque white. Remove both sections. Cut through the center of the chicken to separate both halves. You will probably hear a small snap as you cut through the wishbone. You now have two halves.

TO PREPARE A CHICKEN FOR BROILING

If you are going to broil the chicken, turn each section over skin side up. Place the leg and thighbone up over the bottom section of the breast. By placing the chicken in this position, you protect the lower end of the breast from overcooking. If desired, marinate before cooking.

TO PREPARE À LA CRAPAUDINE

Chickens can also be prepared *à la crapaudine*, or frog style. Instead of cutting the chicken in half lengthwise, leave it whole, with the breastbone removed. Open it like a book and turn it skin side up. Cut a small slit on either side of the skin at the bottom of the chicken and slip the end of each leg into a slit. Press on the chicken to flatten it. The chicken will be almost the same thickness all over. You can make a stuffing and insert it between the skin and the flesh.

TO CUT UP A CHICKEN FOR SAUTÉING

Turn the chicken skin side up after cutting it in half lengthwise along the breastbone. With a knife held at an angle, cut toward the leg to separate the breast and leg. The object is to leave as much skin as possible on the breast, to protect it during cooking. With the heel of the knife, make a sharp, quick chop about 1 inch from the knuckle of the leg. This can be left on, but all it does is take up room in the pan. If you chop it off, you can add it to the other sections to make stock. With a small knife, carefully cut through the flesh at the "knee" to separate the thigh and the leg. The object is to separate them without chopping into the bone and making fragments. They will separate if you cut through the cartilage. If you did not succeed in cutting through the backbone on the first two cuts, there may be a section of hipbone attached to the thigh, which happens about half of the time. With a small knife, cut through the cartilage and separate the hipbone. You now have a leg and a thigh each with a bone down the center.

Pull the rib cage off the inside of the breast. It comes off easily. With a knife, cut through the elbow of the wing. Use the forearm and wing tip for stock; or separate them and use the tip for stock, keeping the forearm, or second section, to barbecue as a snack or, if you have enough of them, as a main course. Feel around the upper end of the breast and find a tiny little bone, the wishbone. Push off the flesh with your fingers and pull it out of the shoulder socket. If it is the "lucky" side, you may have to cut around the end. Discard the bone. There is also a flat bone that you can release by pushing off the flesh or by cutting underneath with a small knife. Twist that bone out of the shoulder socket and discard. The breast has a bone down the upper arm and a bone down the center of the breast. If you want boneless fillets, separate the arm at the shoulder and then pull out the remaining bone. The upper arm can be used in any chicken wing recipe. The breast can be cut in half crosswise to make two portions, but I usually leave it whole. The foregoing method produces six pieces of chicken, which I consider to be four servings: two breast servings and two servings of a leg and a thigh each.

An aside on sautéing chickens: Many authors tell you to remove the breasts 5 minutes before the legs and thighs have finished cooking so that the breasts will not overcook. I recommend that you cook the thighs and legs about 5 minutes before you add the breasts to the skillet. Then they will all be done when you are most in need of time to finish a sauce and assemble the rest of the meal.

SAUCE THICKENERS

There are three thickeners used for the sauces in these recipes: flour, cornstarch, and potato starch. Flour has the least amount of thickening ability. It also gives the sauce a somewhat cloudy, although not disagreeable, appearance. If you substitute cornstarch or potato starch, the sauce will look clearer. However, you need to use about twice as much flour as you would potato starch or cornstarch, which have similar thickening ability. On a boat, where storage is a problem, I would select just one thickener (or two at most) to use. Flour would be the thickener of choice since you would normally stock it.

Thickeners are generally added at the end of the cooking time. To use them, make a slurry. Mix the thickener with the same amount of water, or a little more, to make a pourable mixture. Add this to the simmering liquid, stirring constantly, and cook until thickened and smooth.

Chicken with Rosemary and Lemon

INGREDIENTS:

ONE 2½-POUND CHICKEN
   CUT UP FOR SAUTÉING

4 TABLESPOONS BUTTER

3 TABLESPOONS COGNAC

1 CLOVE GARLIC, CRUSHED

1 TO 1½ CUPS CHICKEN
   STOCK

¼ CUP DRY WHITE WINE

½ TEASPOON TOMATO PASTE

2 TEASPOONS POTATO
   STARCH

JUICE AND GRATED RIND
   OF 1 LEMON

½ TEASPOON ROSEMARY

SALT AND PEPPER TO TASTE

☐ In a skillet, brown the chicken in 3 tablespoons of the butter.

☐ Pour on the Cognac and ignite. When the flames die down, remove the chicken and set aside.

☐ Add the remaining tablespoon of butter to the pan and lightly brown the garlic. Blend in the chicken stock, wine, tomato paste, potato starch, lemon juice, lemon rind, and rosemary. Bring to a simmer, stirring. Correct seasoning with salt and pepper.

☐ Return the chicken to the skillet, cover, and simmer 15 to 20 minutes or until tender.

YIELDS 4 SERVINGS.

Poulet Sauté à la Portugaise

Sautéed Chicken Portuguese Style

☐ Dredge the chicken in flour seasoned with salt and pepper.

☐ In a skillet, heat the butter and brown the chicken on both sides, about 15 minutes.

☐ Add the shallots and cook until soft, but not brown.

☐ Stir in the flour, garlic, wine, stock, and cooked tomatoes. Simmer 10 minutes.

☐ Add the fresh tomatoes and simmer 10 minutes longer.

☐ Arrange on a platter and sprinkle with parsley.

YIELDS 4 SERVINGS.

INGREDIENTS:

ONE 2½-POUND CHICKEN, CUT UP FOR SAUTÉING

½ CUP FLOUR

SALT AND PEPPER TO TASTE

2 TABLESPOONS CLARIFIED BUTTER

1 TABLESPOON MINCED SHALLOTS

1 TEASPOON FLOUR

1 CLOVE GARLIC, CRUSHED

¼ CUP DRY WHITE WINE

½ CUP CHICKEN STOCK

½ CUP COOKED TOMATOES

4 TO 6 TOMATOES, PEELED, SEEDED, AND CHOPPED

1 TABLESPOON MINCED PARSLEY

Poulet Sauté Normandie

Sautéed Chicken Normandy Style

☐ Season the chicken with salt and pepper.

☐ In a skillet, sauté the onions and chicken in the butter until the chicken is pale golden.

☐ Stir in the flour and add the cider, Calvados, thyme, and chicken stock. Simmer 15 minutes. Add the mushrooms and simmer 10 minutes. Remove the chicken and vegetables to a platter and keep warm.

☐ Add the apples to the skillet and cook over high heat until reduced to the desired consistency. Add the heavy cream and return the chicken and vegetables to the pan. Heat and serve.

YIELDS 4 SERVINGS.

INGREDIENTS:

ONE 2½-POUND CHICKEN, CUT UP FOR SAUTÉING

SALT AND PEPPER TO TASTE

6 SMALL WHITE ONIONS

3 TABLESPOONS CLARIFIED BUTTER

1 TABLESPOON FLOUR

1½ CUPS CIDER

2 TABLESPOONS CALVADOS OR APPLEJACK

SPRIG OF THYME

1½ CUPS CHICKEN STOCK

¼ POUND MUSHROOMS, HALVED

2 APPLES, PEELED, CORED, AND CHOPPED

¼ CUP HEAVY CREAM

Poulet Mallorca

Sauteed Chicken with Tarragon, Peppers, and Oranges

INGREDIENTS:

ONE 2½-POUND CHICKEN, CUT UP FOR SAUTÉING

FLOUR

SALT AND PEPPER TO TASTE

4 TABLESPOONS CLARIFIED BUTTER

1 CLOVE GARLIC, CRUSHED

¼ CUP MADEIRA

1 TEASPOON MEAT GLAZE (OPTIONAL)

4 TEASPOONS POTATO STARCH OR CORNSTARCH

1 CUP CHICKEN STOCK

½ CUP DRY WHITE WINE

1 TEASPOON DRIED TARRAGON

1 TABLESPOON MINCED PARSLEY

3 TABLESPOONS OLIVE OIL

¼ POUND MUSHROOMS, SLICED

2 TEASPOONS LEMON JUICE

1 GREEN PEPPER, CUT INTO JULIENNE

1 RED PEPPER, CUT INTO JULIENNE

3 LARGE TOMATOES, PEELED, SEEDED, AND QUARTERED

☐ Dredge the chicken in flour seasoned with salt and pepper.

☐ In a large skillet, over moderate heat, sauté the chicken in the butter until golden on the skin side. Turn the chicken, add the garlic, and cook until golden, being careful not to burn the garlic. Remove the chicken from the skillet.

☐ Stir in the Madeira, meat glaze, potato starch, chicken stock, white wine, tarragon, and parsley. Simmer, stirring, until thickened and smooth.

☐ Return the chicken to the pan and simmer 15 minutes, partially covered.

☐ Meanwhile, in another skillet, sauté the mushrooms and lemon juice in the olive oil for 2 minutes, add the peppers, and cook over moderate heat until tender.

☐ Drain the tomatoes in a sieve for 10 minutes.

☐ Cut the oranges into segments, discarding the membrane. When the chicken is cooked, remove to a platter.

☐ Add to the chicken skillet with the tomatoes and orange the mushroom-pepper mixture and cook over moderate heat until hot. Pour over the chicken.

YIELDS 4 SERVINGS.

Poulet à la Moutarde
Sautéed Chicken with Mustard Sauce

☐ Season the chicken with salt and pepper.

☐ In a skillet, sauté the chicken in the butter until brown on both sides. Pour off the excess fat and add the carrots, mushrooms, and shallots. Sauté about 4 minutes, sprinkle with flour and stir to distribute.

☐ Stir in the stock, wine, bay leaf, and thyme. Cover and simmer for 20 minutes.

☐ Turn off the heat, remove the chicken to a serving platter, and stir the mustard into the pan. Do not boil.

YIELDS 4 SERVINGS.

INGREDIENTS:
ONE 2½-POUND CHICKEN, CUT UP FOR SAUTÉING
SALT AND PEPPER TO TASTE
2 TABLESPOONS BUTTER
12 SMALL CARROTS
½ POUND SMALL MUSHROOMS
2 TABLESPOONS MINCED SHALLOTS
2 TEASPOONS FLOUR
1 CUP CHICKEN STOCK
1 BAY LEAF
½ TEASPOON DRIED THYME
2 TABLESPOONS DIJON MUSTARD

Poulet Sauté aux Olives
Chicken Sautéed with Olives

☐ Season the chicken with salt and pepper. Brown in a skillet in the butter. Remove the chicken.

☐ Add the mushrooms, shallots, and garlic to the skillet and cook, stirring, for 2 minutes.

☐ Add the wine and tomato purée and cook for 3 minutes. Add the chicken stock, stirring to dissolve any browned bits. Return the chicken to the pan, cover, and simmer 15 minutes.

☐ Add the olives and simmer 15 minutes longer, covered.

☐ Sprinkle with parsley and serve.

YIELDS 4 SERVINGS.

INGREDIENTS:
ONE 2½-POUND CHICKEN, CUT UP FOR SAUTÉING
SALT AND PEPPER TO TASTE
4 TABLESPOONS BUTTER
¼ POUND BUTTON MUSHROOMS
¼ CUP MINCED SHALLOTS
½ TEASPOON MINCED GARLIC
1 CUP WHITE WINE
¼ CUP TOMATO PURÉE
½ CUP CHICKEN STOCK
18 SMALL PITTED GREEN OLIVES OR SMALL OIL-CURED BLACK OLIVES
MINCED PARSLEY

Poulet Dauphinoise
Sautéed Chicken with Garlic and Rosemary

INGREDIENTS:

½ CUP GARLIC CLOVES

ONE 2½-POUND CHICKEN, CUT UP FOR SAUTÉING

FLOUR

SALT AND PEPPER TO TASTE

5 TABLESPOONS CLARIFIED BUTTER

1 TEASPOON DRIED ROSEMARY

1 BAY LEAF

1 TABLESPOON MINCED PARSLEY

LEMON JUICE TO TASTE

☐ Cook the garlic cloves in boiling water to cover for 1 minute. Drain, run under cold water, and slip off the skins. For this dish, it is important that you not bruise the garlic.

☐ Flour the chicken and season with salt and pepper. In a skillet, brown the chicken on both sides in the butter. Push the chicken to one side of the pan and add the garlic cloves, rosemary, and bay leaf. Arrange the chicken skin side up over the garlic, and cook, half covered, over very low heat for 30 to 40 minutes. Baste often with pan juices.

☐ Remove the chicken to a platter and sprinkle with minced parsley. Mash the cooked garlic in the pan juices and whisk in the lemon juice, salt, and pepper. Pour over the chicken.

YIELDS 4 SERVINGS.

Grilled Chicken

Try mixing a clove of crushed garlic and a dash or two of Tabasco sauce into the oil. Use any herb you like. Oregano and tarragon are other favorites.

INGREDIENTS:

2 BROILERS, CUT FOR BROILING

1 LEMON, CUT IN HALF

SALT AND PEPPER TO TASTE

1 TABLESPOON THYME, MARJORAM, OR SAVORY

½ CUP OLIVE OIL

¼ CUP BUTTER, MELTED

☐ Rub the chicken with lemon and season with salt, pepper, and the herb of your choice. Place in a pan and brush with the olive oil. Let marinate an hour or more.

☐ When the chicken is ready to broil, place it skin side up on a broiler rack, brush with butter, and broil 15 minutes. Brush twice during broiling. Turn and broil 10 minutes longer or until the meat is cooked, brushing with more butter. Season with salt.

YIELDS 4 SERVINGS.

Poulet Sauté Bercy

Sautéed Chicken with White Wine Sauce

This is a basic sauté recipe that can be used for fish, beef, lamb, veal, or pork. If you prefer, add ½ cup tomato sauce with the wine or ¼ pound sliced mushrooms with the shallots. For Poulet Sauté Bordelaise, substitute red wine for the white.

☐ Dredge the chicken in flour seasoned with salt and pepper. In a skillet, brown the chicken on both sides in the butter until done. Remove to a platter and keep warm.

☐ Add the shallots and flour to the skillet and cook, stirring, for 1 minute. Add the wine, stock, and tomato sauce. Cook, stirring up any browned bits, until the sauce is of the desired consistency. Correct the seasoning with salt and pepper. Pour over the chicken and sprinkle with the parsley.

YIELDS 4 SERVINGS.

INGREDIENTS:

ONE 2½-POUND CHICKEN, CUT UP FOR SAUTÉING

FLOUR

SALT AND PEPPER TO TASTE

3 TABLESPOONS CLARIFIED BUTTER

1 TABLESPOON MINCED SHALLOTS

1 TEASPOON FLOUR

¼ CUP WHITE WINE

¼ CUP CHICKEN STOCK

3 TABLESPOONS TOMATO SAUCE

MINCED PARSLEY

Broiled Rosemary Lemon Chicken

You can add further interest to this recipe by inserting rounds of goat cheese, such as Montrachet, between the skin and the flesh of the chicken before marinating. For even more flavor, insert a section of oil-preserved, sun-dried tomato in each section.

☐ In a bowl, combine the olive oil, lemon juice, garlic, bay leaves, rosemary, salt, and pepper, and mix well.

☐ Arrange the chicken in a flat dish and pour the marinade over it. Let marinate in a cool spot for up to 12 hours.

☐ Broil, basting often with the marinade.

YIELDS 4 SERVINGS.

INGREDIENTS:

1 CUP OLIVE OIL

JUICE OF 3 LEMONS

3 GARLIC CLOVES, MINCED

3 BAY LEAVES

1 TABLESPOON ROSEMARY

1 TEASPOON SALT

½ TEASPOON GROUND PEPPER

2 BROILERS, CUT UP FOR BROILING

Poulet Sauté à La Basquaise

Sautéed Chicken Basque Style

INGREDIENTS:

ONE 2½-POUND CHICKEN,
 CUT UP FOR SAUTÉING

SALT AND PEPPER TO TASTE

2 TABLESPOONS BUTTER

2 TABLESPOONS OLIVE OIL

1 ONION, MINCED

5 TO 6 GREEN PEPPERS,
 SEEDED AND CHOPPED

4 TABLESPOONS COGNAC

½ CUP DRY WHITE WINE

3 TOMATOES, PEELED,
 SEEDED, AND CHOPPED

4 OUNCES PROSCIUTTO,
 CUT INTO JULIENNE

4 OUNCES CHORIZO, SLICED
 AND FRIED IN 2 TABLE-
 SPOONS BUTTER

☐ Season the chicken with salt and pepper.

☐ In a large skillet, heat the oil and butter and brown the chicken on both sides. When it is cooked through, remove to a platter and keep warm.

☐ Add the onion and peppers and cook, stirring, for 5 minutes over medium heat.

☐ Add the cognac, wine, and tomatoes and cook over high heat until thickened.

☐ Arrange the chicken on a platter and pour the sauce over it. Garnish with the prosciutto and chorizo.

YIELDS 4 SERVINGS.

Chicken Cutlets Parmesan

INGREDIENTS:

4 BONELESS CHICKEN
 BREASTS

¼ CUP FLOUR

2 EGGS

3 TABLESPOONS MILK

1½ CUPS FRESH BREAD
 CRUMBS

1 CUP GRATED PARMESAN
 CHEESE

⅓ CUP OLIVE OIL

2 LEMONS, QUARTERED

☐ Remove the white tendon from each chicken breast half. Dust well with flour.

☐ In a bowl, beat the eggs and milk together.

☐ In a pie tin, mix the crumbs and cheese. The crumb mixture can be flavored with various herbs, such as dried oregano, rosemary, savory, etc. If you prefer, mix in a generous pinch of curry powder or sprinkle in a little cayenne pepper.

☐ Dip each floured cutlet first into the egg mixture and then into the crumbs, pressing firmly to help them adhere. Place on a baking sheet and let stand for 45 minutes to 1 hour.

☐ Heat the olive oil in a skillet and sauté the cutlets until golden on each side. Do not crowd the cutlets.

☐ Can be served hot or cold, with lemon wedges.

YIELDS 4 TO 8 SERVINGS.

Poulet Sauté aux Artichauts
Sautéed Chicken with Artichokes

☐ Dredge the chicken in flour seasoned with salt and pepper.

☐ In a skillet, brown the chicken in the clarified butter until both sides are golden. Remove the chicken and set aside.

☐ Brown the shallots in the pan, return the chicken, and add the bay leaf. Cook, covered, over low heat for 25 to 30 minutes, basting often.

☐ Meanwhile, in a saucepan, toss the artichokes in the melted butter and lemon juice until well coated. Season with salt and cook, covered, over low heat for 10 minutes.

☐ Remove the chicken to a platter. Arrange the shallots around the chicken.

☐ Add the stock to the skillet and cook, stirring up the browned bits, until reduced to ½ cup. Season to taste and pour over the chicken. Place the artichokes on the platter and sprinkle with the minced parsley.

YIELDS 4 SERVINGS.

INGREDIENTS:

ONE 2½-POUND CHICKEN, CUT UP FOR SAUTÉING

SALT AND PEPPER TO TASTE

FLOUR

3 TABLESPOONS CLARIFIED BUTTER, SEE PAGE 178

16 LARGE SHALLOTS, PEELED

1 BAY LEAF

10 OUNCES FROZEN ARTICHOKE HEARTS

2 TABLESPOONS BUTTER

1 TEASPOON LEMON JUICE

1 CUP CHICKEN STOCK

2 TABLESPOONS MINCED PARSLEY

Chicken with Clams and Spaghetti

INGREDIENTS:

ONE 2½-POUND CHICKEN,
    CUT UP FOR SAUTÉING
SALT AND PEPPER TO TASTE
¼ POUND BUTTER
¼ TEASPOON DRIED THYME
¼ CUP MINCED SHALLOTS
1 CUP HEAVY CREAM
½ CUP GRATED PARMESAN
    CHEESE
¾ CUP FRESHLY OPENED
    CLAMS, CHOPPED
¾ CUP CLAM JUICE
¾ POUND SPAGHETTI
2 TEASPOONS MINCED
    GARLIC
2 TEASPOONS MINCED
    FRESH BASIL
2 TEASPOONS MINCED
    PARSLEY

☐ Season the chicken with salt and pepper.

☐ In a skillet, sauté the chicken in 2 tablespoons of butter until both sides are golden. Sprinkle with thyme and shallots, cover, and cook 15 minutes longer. Add the cream, cover, and simmer 10 minutes.

☐ Chop the clams and set aside.

☐ In a kettle, bring 2 quarts of water to a boil and add the clam juice. Cook the spaghetti in the water until *al dente*.

☐ In a small saucepan, melt 2 tablespoons of the butter and cook the garlic, basil, and parsley for 1 minute. Add the clams and cook, stirring, for 1 minute or until heated. Season with salt and pepper.

☐ Drain the pasta and put into a bowl. Toss with 4 tablespoons of butter. Add the clam mixture and toss with grated cheese and a goodly amount of black pepper. Pour the chicken and its sauce over all.

YIELDS 6 SERVINGS.

Coq au Citron
Braised Chicken with Lemon

INGREDIENTS:

1 CHICKEN, CUT UP FOR
    SAUTÉING
4 TABLESPOONS BUTTER
1 TABLESPOON FLOUR
1 CUP CHICKEN STOCK
BOUQUET GARNI OF THYME,
    PARSLEY, AND BAY LEAF
1 LARGE LEMON, DICED
1 LEMON, SLICED

☐ In a skillet, brown the chicken in the butter and remove to a platter.

☐ Stir the flour into the skillet and cook 2 minutes or until golden brown. Add the chicken stock and bouquet garni with the diced lemon. Cook, stirring up any browned bits.

☐ Add the chicken and turn over in the sauce. Cover and simmer over low heat for 30 minutes, turning occasionally.

☐ Remove the chicken to a platter and strain the sauce over it. Garnish with fresh lemon slices.

YIELDS 4 SERVINGS.

Pollo Arrabbiato
Chicken with Hot Chili Sauce

- Soak the mushrooms in hot water to cover for at least 30 minutes.

- Season the chicken with salt and pepper to taste.

- In a saucepan, reduce the tomatoes over medium heat to 1 cup, stirring often.

- In a large skillet, sauté the chicken in the olive oil until both sides are golden, add the salami, and heat through. Remove the chicken and salami to a platter and keep warm.

- Pour off the fat from the skillet and add the garlic. Add the wine and reduce by half. Add the cooked-down tomatoes.

- Drain the mushrooms, reserving ½ cup of soaking liquid.

- Add the mushrooms and reserved liquid to the sauce, with the crushed red pepper flakes and the chicken. Cook until the chicken is done, about 10 minutes. Stir in the salami and correct seasoning with salt and pepper to taste.

- Sprinkle with parsley and serve.

YIELDS 4 SERVINGS.

INGREDIENTS:

1 OUNCE DRIED ITALIAN MUSHROOMS

ONE 3-POUND CHICKEN, CUT UP FOR SAUTÉING

SALT AND PEPPER TO TASTE

2 CUPS CANNED TOMATOES

3 TABLESPOONS OLIVE OIL

8 THIN SLICES GENOA SALAMI, CUT INTO JULIENNE

1 TEASPOON MINCED GARLIC

½ CUP WHITE WINE

1 TEASPOON CRUSHED RED PEPPER FLAKES

MINCED PARSLEY

Poulet Grillé au Persil

Garlic-and-Parsley-Coated Grilled Chicken

INGREDIENTS:

1 BROILER, CUT UP FOR BROILING

SALT AND PEPPER TO TASTE

4 TABLESPOONS BUTTER, SOFTENED

1 CUP FRESH BREAD CRUMBS

¼ CUP MINCED PARSLEY

1 CLOVE GARLIC, MINCED

☐ Season the chicken pieces with salt and pepper and rub with 2 tablespoons of the butter.

☐ Broil about 12 minutes on each side or until done.

☐ In a bowl, combine the remaining butter, bread crumbs, parsley, garlic, salt, and pepper. The mixture should have the consistency of damp sand. If necessary, add a little more butter.

☐ When the chicken is cooked, press a handful of the bread crumb mixture onto each piece in an even layer. Expect some to fall off. (For additional flavor, brush the chicken with Dijon mustard before pressing on the bread crumbs.)

☐ Broil about 2 minutes under the broiler until the crumbs are golden.

YIELDS 2 SERVINGS.

Cornish Hens à la Crapaudine

If sherry vinegar is not available, use a mild-flavored vinegar such as balsamic, or even lemon juice, rather than a very acidic wine or cider vinegar.

INGREDIENTS:

4 ROCK CORNISH HENS

SALT AND PEPPER TO TASTE

¼ CUP OLIVE OIL

2 TABLESPOONS SHERRY VINEGAR

1 CLOVE GARLIC, MINCED

¼ TEASPOON DRIED THYME

¼ TEASPOON DRIED SAGE

¼ TEASPOON DRIED BASIL

☐ Split the hens down the backbone and prepare *à la crapaudine*, as described on page 74.

☐ Transfer hens to a flat dish and season with salt and pepper.

☐ In a small bowl, beat together the olive oil, vinegar, garlic, thyme, sage, and basil leaves. Pour this mixture over the hens and rub in well. Let marinate for about 4 hours.

☐ Grill the hens until done, basting often with the marinade.

YIELDS 4 SERVINGS.

Poulet Grillé à la Diable

Devilled Grilled Chicken

☐ Season the chicken with salt and pepper to taste. Rub with 2 tablespoons of the butter.

☐ Broil about 12 minutes on each side or until cooked.

☐ In a bowl, combine the remaining butter, bread crumbs, mustard, cayenne, and Worcestershire sauce. The mixture should have the consistency of damp sand. If necessary, add a little more butter. (This mixture can also be flavored to taste with an herb of your choice, such as oregano or marjoram. Try adding some mashed anchovies or anchovy paste, or season the bread crumbs with ¼ teaspoon of curry powder or more to the bread crumb mixture. This coating works well on fish, pork chops or lamb steaks as well as chicken.)

☐ When the chicken pieces are done, press a handful of bread crumbs onto them in an even layer. Don't worry if some of the bread crumbs fall off. Broil the chicken for about 2 minutes or until the crumbs are golden.

YIELDS 2 SERVINGS.

INGREDIENTS:

1 BROILER, CUT UP FOR BROILING

SALT AND PEPPER TO TASTE

4 TABLESPOONS BUTTER, SOFTENED

1 CUP FRESH BREAD CRUMBS

1 TEASPOON DRY MUSTARD

PINCH OF CAYENNE PEPPER

WORCESTERSHIRE SAUCE

Chasha Shamdeh

Tibetan Curried Chicken

INGREDIENTS:

3 TABLESPOONS VEGETABLE OIL

¾ CUP MINCED ONION

1 TABLESPOON MINCED GINGERROOT

2 TEASPOONS MINCED GARLIC

3 CORNISH GAME HENS, HALVED

1 TEASPOON SALT

1 TEASPOON TURMERIC

½ TEASPOON DRIED RED PEPPER FLAKES

¼ TEASPOON PEPPER

1 CUP WATER

☐ In a large skillet, sauté the onion, ginger, and garlic in the oil for 3 minutes. Add the hens and sprinkle them with salt, turmeric, pepper flakes, and pepper. Brown on all sides, scraping the bottom of the skillet to prevent the vegetables from sticking.

☐ Add the water, cover, and simmer until the hens are tender, about 30 minutes.

YIELDS 6 SERVINGS.

Chicken Liver Brochettes in Sage Butter

INGREDIENTS:

18 BUTTON MUSHROOMS

4 TABLESPOONS OLIVE OIL

4 TABLESPOONS BUTTER

18 SLICES OF BREAD, 1½ INCHES SQUARE

SAGE BUTTER, SEE FACING PAGE

SALT AND PEPPER TO TASTE

1 POUND CHICKEN LIVERS, HALVED

☐ Preheat the broiler.

☐ Place the mushrooms in a baking dish, season with salt and pepper, and drizzle with 2 tablespoons of the olive oil.

☐ Broil for 2 minutes and set aside.

☐ In a skillet, heat the butter and cook the chicken livers until firm, but not cooked through. Season with salt and pepper.

☐ Add the remaining 2 tablespoons of olive oil to the skillet and sauté the bread squares until golden. Set aside.

☐ On skewers, thread the bread squares, livers, and mushrooms, alternating. Dot with the sage butter and broil for 2 minutes, turning twice.

☐ Serve remaining butter on the side.

YIELDS 6 SERVINGS.

Sage Butter

This butter can be used for chicken or fish. Substitute another herb for the sage, if desired.

☐ In a bowl, mash the butter until smooth, then mash in the sage, parsley, and shallots.

YIELDS ½ CUP.

INGREDIENTS:

6 TABLESPOONS BUTTER, SOFTENED

2 TABLESPOONS MINCED SAGE

2 TABLESPOONS MINCED PARSLEY

2 SHALLOTS, MINCED

Chicken and Rice Basque Style

☐ Season the chicken with salt and pepper.

☐ In a large skillet or casserole, heat 3 tablespoons of the olive oil, sauté the chicken livers for 3 minutes, season with salt and pepper, and set aside.

☐ Add the remaining 2 tablespoons of olive oil to the skillet and sauté the chicken pieces until both sides are golden, about 15 minutes. Remove and set aside.

☐ Add the onion, garlic, and chili pepper, and cook, stirring, for 5 minutes. Add the green peppers, red peppers, and parsley, and cook, stirring, for 3 minutes. Add the tomatoes and bring to a boil. Season with salt and pepper.

☐ Add the chicken, lower the heat, and simmer 10 minutes.

☐ Add the rice, peas, and chicken livers. Return to a boil and add the chicken stock. Simmer over very low heat, covered, for 17 minutes. Remove and discard the chili pepper.

YIELDS 6 SERVINGS.

INGREDIENTS:

ONE 2½-POUND CHICKEN, CUT UP FOR SAUTÉING

SALT AND PEPPER TO TASTE

5 TABLESPOONS OLIVE OIL

4 CHICKEN LIVERS, CUT IN HALF

1 CUP MINCED ONION

2 GARLIC CLOVES, CRUSHED

1 SMALL, HOT, DRIED CHILI PEPPER

1 CUP MINCED GREEN PEPPER

½ CUP MINCED RED PEPPER

¼ CUP MINCED PARSLEY

1 CAN (32 OUNCES) ITALIAN-STYLE PLUM TOMATOES, DRAINED

1 CUP RICE

1 CUP PEAS, FRESH OR FROZEN

1¾ CUPS CHICKEN STOCK

Poulet en Cocotte Grandmère

Braised Stuffed Chicken

INGREDIENTS:

3 SHALLOTS, MINCED
¼ CUP BUTTER
½ POUND HAM, GROUND OR MINCED
1 CUP FRESH BREAD CRUMBS
1 TEASPOON THYME
SALT AND PEPPER TO TASTE
1 EGG
ONE 4-POUND CHICKEN
3 TABLESPOONS BUTTER
¼ CUP DRY SHERRY
BOUQUET GARNI
3 OUNCES DICED SALT PORK
12 SMALL ONIONS, PEELED
1 POUND SMALL POTATOES
1 CUP CHICKEN STOCK
1 TABLESPOON CORNSTARCH
1 TEASPOON MINCED PARSLEY
½ TEASPOON MINCED THYME
½ TEASPOON MINCED BASIL

☐ Preheat the oven to 350°F.

☐ In a skillet, sauté the shallots in the butter until soft. Add the ham, bread crumbs, thyme, salt, pepper, and egg. Stuff and truss the chicken.

☐ In a casserole or deep skillet, brown the chicken on all sides in the 3 tablespoons of butter. Drain off the excess fat and reserve it.

☐ Add the sherry and the bouquet garni to the pan with the chicken and cook over moderate heat on top of the stove, or in a 350°F oven, for 30 minutes or until tender.

☐ Meanwhile, blanch the pork, onions, and potatoes in boiling water for 4 minutes. Drain well.

☐ In the reserved butter, brown the pork, onions, and potatoes, and add them to the chicken about 5 minutes before the end of the cooking. Remove the chicken to a serving platter and surround it with vegetables.

☐ Add the stock to the skillet or casserole, and bring to a boil.

☐ In a small bowl, combine the cornstarch with 2 tablespoons of cold water. Stir into the simmering sauce and add the parsley, thyme, and basil. Serve with the chicken.

YIELDS 4 TO 6 SERVINGS.

Poulet en Casserole à la Béarnaise

Casserole of Chicken Béarnaise

☐ In a small bowl, mash the butter and 1 tablespoon of the tarragon together. Rub the inside of the chicken with the butter. Truss the chicken.

☐ In a casserole, place the chicken, chicken stock, carrots, onions, clove, salt, and pepper. Bring to a boil and lower the heat. Simmer 40 minutes. Remove the chicken to a platter and keep warm. Reduce the cooking liquid by half.

☐ In a bowl, combine the flour, the remaining tarragon, and cream. Whisk into the simmering stock and cook, stirring, until slightly thickened. Correct seasoning with salt and pepper. Serve with rice.

INGREDIENTS:

2½ TABLESPOONS BUTTER

2 TABLESPOONS DRIED TARRAGON

ONE 4-POUND CHICKEN

1 QUART CHICKEN STOCK

2 CARROTS, SLICED

2 SMALL ONIONS, SLICED

1 CLOVE

SALT AND PEPPER TO TASTE

1 TABLESPOON FLOUR

3 TABLESPOONS HEAVY CREAM

BOILED RICE

YIELDS 4 TO 6 SERVINGS.

Waterzooi

Poached Chicken with Egg and Cream Sauce

☐ In a heavy casserole, sweat the celery, leeks, mushrooms, 2 tablespoons of the butter, and parsley, covered, for 10 minutes.

☐ Truss the chicken and place it in the casserole. Season with salt and pepper, and add the remaining butter and the wine. Cover tightly and cook over very low heat for 1¼ hours or until the chicken is tender. Do not let the vegetables brown. When the chicken is done, remove it to a platter.

☐ Beat the egg yolks with the cream and add them to the vegetables, stirring well. Correct seasoning with salt and pepper. Cook over low heat, stirring, until the sauce just thickens. Do not let it boil. Pour over the chicken and serve at once with rice.

INGREDIENTS:

2 CUPS THINLY SLICED CELERY

2 LEEKS, THINLY SLICED

¼ POUND MUSHROOMS, THINLY SLICED

4 TABLESPOONS BUTTER

LARGE SPRIG OF PARSLEY

ONE 4-POUND ROASTING CHICKEN

SALT AND PEPPER TO TASTE

½ CUP DRY WHITE WINE

4 EGG YOLKS

1 CUP HEAVY CREAM

YIELDS 6 SERVINGS.

Poulet en Cocotte Bonne Femme

Braised Chicken with Vegetables

INGREDIENTS:
ONE 3½-POUND CHICKEN
4 TABLESPOONS BUTTER
¼ TEASPOON MINCED GARLIC
½ TEASPOON DRIED THYME
¼ POUND SALT PORK, DICED
SPRIG OF PARSLEY
BAY LEAF
5 TABLESPOONS BUTTER
16 SMALL WHITE ONIONS
6 CARROTS, CUT INTO
  2-INCH CYLINDERS
16 TINY NEW POTATOES OR
  POTATO BALLS
SALT AND PEPPER TO TASTE

☐ Preheat the oven to 350°F.

☐ In a bowl, mash the 4 tablespoons of butter with the garlic and thyme, and spread over the inside of the chicken. Rub 2 tablespoons of butter over the surface of chicken.

☐ Blanch the salt pork in boiling salted water for 5 minutes and drain. Melt 1 tablespoon of butter in a skillet and brown the blanched pork, stirring, until crisp and golden. Set aside.

☐ Brown the chicken in the fat in the pan. Place a thin film of fat in a casserole and add the chicken and pork. Cook over medium heat until the fat begins to splutter and place in the oven, covered. Cook for 45 minutes, basting twice with the accumulated juices.

☐ In the skillet, melt the remaining 2 tablespoons of butter and cook the onions, carrots, and potatoes until coated with butter and lightly colored. When the 45 minutes are up, add the vegetables to the chicken, along with the parsley and bay leaf, and braise 30 minutes longer.

☐ Arrange the chicken and vegetables on a platter. Discard the parsley and bay leaf. Remove any fat from the juices and serve these with chicken.

YIELDS 4 TO 6 SERVINGS.

SIX

MEATS

Although it is possible to use most methods of cooking meat on a boat, it is usually best to sauté or to broil. Veal, pork, or lamb can be braised. Roasting and preparing braised dishes from the tougher cuts of meat require too much time – save them for when you are at home.

Any broiled meat can be enhanced by one of the composed butters listed in the chapter for basic sauces. These provide a hint of sauce to create the elegance of fine dining without putting you through hours of serious labor. In addition, they are far less tricky to prepare than a hollandaise or béarnaise sauce. You *can* prepare those sauces in a galley but why go to all that trouble? Especially when you may have a greater need for stove space to cook vegetables, or a soup.

Steaks, chops, and cutlets are all suitable cuts to take on a cruise. Freeze them separately and then take out as many as you need for a particular meal. Many of the sauces and preparations for chicken or fish can be used for beef, lamb, pork, or veal. Certainly, many of the suggestions for sautéed chicken work equally well with red meats. To economize, use hamburger and one of the sauces suggested for steak or chicken. A dish *à la forestière* is named for the sauce, not the meat. The sauce will work well with steak, hamburger, chicken, lamb, or veal, and there is no reason why it cannot accompany a firm-fleshed fish or even shrimp. Not traditional, certainly, but very good to eat.

Avoid larger pieces of meat such as rib roasts and legs of lamb. Both have large bones and require too much storage space. Also, even cooked rare, they use too much fuel. Smaller cuts are easier to store and more versatile.

Ground beef can be cooked as hamburgers or prepared with one of the sauces or composed butters. It is also very handy to have for meatballs. Make tiny ones for cocktails or larger ones for a main course. Since meatloaf takes time and fuel to cook, try making several large meatballs and serving them warm as a main course or using them cooled and sliced for sandwiches.

Steak Sautéed in Scotch and Tarragon Sauce

INGREDIENTS:

3 TABLESPOONS CLARIFIED BUTTER

1½-POUND SIRLOIN STEAK, 2 INCHES THICK

2 TABLESPOONS BUTTER

½ CUP SCOTCH

1 CUP CHICKEN STOCK

1 TEASPOON GREEN PEPPERCORNS, DRAINED

2 TEASPOONS POTATO STARCH

2 TO 3 TABLESPOONS TARRAGON, MINCED

1½ TEASPOONS SALT

¼ TEASPOON GROUND PEPPER

☐ In a skillet, sauté the steaks in the clarified butter until well browned on both sides and cooked to the desired degree of doneness. Remove to a cutting board.

☐ Remove the fat from the pan, add the 2 tablespoons of butter, and melt over moderately high heat.

☐ Add the Scotch and cook until reduced to a glaze.

☐ Add all but 1 tablespoon of the chicken stock and the green peppercorns. Simmer.

☐ In a small bowl, mix the remaining tablespoon of chicken stock with the potato starch and stir this mixture into the simmering sauce until thickened. Season with tarragon and salt and pepper.

☐ Slice the steak thinly and arrange on a platter. Pour the sauce over all.

YIELDS 4 SERVINGS.

Entrecôte à la Forestiere
Sirloin Steak with Mushrooms

Ground beef, chicken, fish, lamb, pork, or veal can be substituted for the steaks.

☐ In a skillet, sauté the steaks in the butter to the desired degree of doneness. Remove steaks to a platter and keep warm.

☐ Add the mushrooms to the skillet and cook until tender.

☐ Add the wine and cook, scraping up any browned bits, until reduced by half. Season sauce with salt and pepper to taste. Sprinkle with parsley and pour over the steaks.

INGREDIENTS:
4 SIRLOIN STEAKS
4 TABLESPOONS CLARIFIED BUTTER, SEE PAGE 178
½ POUND MUSHROOMS, SLICED
½ CUP DRY WHITE WINE
SALT AND PEPPER TO TASTE
2 TABLESPOONS MINCED PARSLEY

YIELDS 4 SERVINGS.

Flank Steak with Tomato Olive Sauce

☐ In a large pan, heat enough water to cover the steak by ½ inch to the point where bubbles start to rise from the bottom.

☐ Add the steak, poach for 5 minutes, turn, and poach 5 minutes longer. The steak should be rare. Do not let the water boil. Remove to a platter, cover, and let cool. Slice thinly.

☐ In a bowl, mix the tomatoes, garlic, olives, shallot, vinegar, oil, pepper, and salt to taste. Let stand for at least 1 hour.

☐ Just before serving, stir in the parsley and serve over the meat slices.

INGREDIENTS:
1½ POUNDS FLANK STEAK
8 CANNED PLUM TOMATOES, CHOPPED AND DRAINED
1 GARLIC CLOVE, MASHED
8 OIL-CURED OLIVES, CHOPPED
1 SHALLOT, MINCED
1 TEASPOON WHITE WINE VINEGAR
3 TABLESPOONS OLIVE OIL
½ TEASPOON PEPPER
SALT
2 TABLESPOONS MINCED PARSLEY

YIELDS 6 SERVINGS.

Bordeaux Beef Stew

Use a relatively tender cut of beef, such as eye of the round, for a cooking time of this length.

INGREDIENTS:

2¾ POUNDS BEEF, CUT INTO
  1½-INCH CUBES
1 CUP RED WINE
1 BAY LEAF
2 CLOVES
2 CLOVES GARLIC
1 TEASPOON SALT
8 PEPPERCORNS
4 SLICES BACON OR FATBACK
2 CUPS BEEF STOCK
8 SPRIGS OF PARSLEY
2 STALKS CELERY
12 CARROT SECTIONS,
  1 INCH LONG
12 SMALL WHITE ONIONS
12 MUSHROOM CAPS
1½ CUPS COOKED PEAS

☐ In a bowl, combine the beef, wine, bay leaf, cloves, 1 clove garlic, salt, and peppercorns. Marinate for 2 hours.

☐ In a skillet, render the bacon over low heat until crisp. Remove. Drain the beef and brown in the skillet with the remaining garlic clove.

☐ Add the marinade and bring to a boil. Add the beef broth, parsley, and celery. Simmer over low heat for 30 minutes.

☐ Add the carrots, onions, and mushrooms, and simmer gently for 1 hour longer or until tender. Add the peas and serve with rice, if desired.

YIELDS 4 TO 6 SERVINGS.

Entrecôte au Roquefort
Sirloin Steak with Roquefort Sauce

INGREDIENTS:

4 RIB EYE STEAKS
4 TABLESPOONS ROQUEFORT
  CHEESE
2 TABLESPOONS MINCED
  PARSLEY
¼ CUP SOFTENED BUTTER
SALT AND PEPPER TO TASTE
LEMON JUICE

☐ Broil the steaks to the desired degree of doneness.

☐ Meanwhile, or several hours before, mash the Roquefort, parsley, and butter together. Season with salt, pepper, and lemon juice. Shape into a roll and cut into slices.

☐ Place a slice of the butter on each cooked steak. This butter can also be used on other meats such as ground beef, veal chops, or lamb steaks.

YIELDS 4 SERVINGS.

Bul Gogi

Korean Grilled Beef Slices

☐ In a bowl, combine the scallions, garlic, soy sauce, peanut oil, sugar, sake, sesame seeds, and pepper.

☐ Add the meat slices and turn to coat. Marinate at least 1 hour. If desired, arrange the meat on skewers or place directly over the grill. Grill to desired degree of doneness.

YIELDS 4 TO 6 SERVINGS.

INGREDIENTS:

6 SCALLIONS, MINCED

5 LARGE GARLIC CLOVES, CRUSHED

½ CUP DARK SOY SAUCE

2 TABLESPOONS PEANUT OIL

2 TABLESPOONS BROWN SUGAR

2 TABLESPOONS SAKE

2 TABLESPOONS TOASTED SESAME SEEDS

PEPPER TO TASTE

2 POUNDS SIRLOIN OR FLANK STEAK, SLICED ¼-INCH THICK ACROSS THE GRAIN

Vienna Steaks

☐ In a bowl, mix together the beef, bacon, onion, 1 egg, cinnamon, garlic, salt, and pepper. Shape into 4 to 6 large flat steaks. Dredge with the flour.

☐ In a bowl, beat the remaining egg and 2 tablespoons of water.

☐ Place the bread crumbs in a pie tin.

☐ Dip the steaks first into the egg and then into the bread crumbs, pressing to coat evenly. Let stand for at least 30 minutes on a rack, if possible.

☐ In a skillet, sauté the steaks in the butter over medium heat until browned on both sides.

YIELDS 4 TO 6 SERVINGS.

INGREDIENTS:

2 POUNDS LEAN GROUND BEEF

2 SLICES BACON, MINCED

½ CUP MINCED ONION

2 EGGS

1 TEASPOON CINNAMON

1 CLOVE GARLIC, CRUSHED

SALT AND PEPPER TO TASTE

FLOUR

2 CUPS FINE BREAD CRUMBS

4 TABLESPOONS BUTTER

Boulets
Meatballs in Cider Tomato Cream Sauce

INGREDIENTS:
1 ONION, DICED
1½ TABLESPOONS BUTTER
1 POUND GROUND BEEF
2 TABLESPOONS MINCED
   PARSLEY
1 EGG
1 CUP HEAVY CREAM
SALT AND PEPPER TO TASTE
5 TABLESPOONS BUTTER
½ CUP CIDER
4 TOMATOES, PEELED,
   SEEDED, AND CHOPPED

☐ In a small skillet, sauté the onion in the butter until soft but not brown.

☐ Stir the onion into the beef, along with the parsley, egg, salt, and pepper. Shape into balls.

☐ Heat the remaining butter in a skillet and sauté the meatballs until golden on all sides.

☐ Add the cider and tomatoes and season with salt and pepper. Simmer for 15 minutes.

☐ Add the cream and simmer 15 minutes longer.

YIELDS 4 SERVINGS.

Grillade Marinière de Valence
Mariner's Meat Ragoût

INGREDIENTS:
2 CUPS MINCED ONION
1-POUND FLANK STEAK,
   CUT INTO 1-INCH CUBES
SALT AND PEPPER TO TASTE
6 TABLESPOONS BUTTER
3 TABLESPOONS FLOUR
4 TO 5 ANCHOVY FILLETS,
   MINCED
2 GARLIC CLOVES, MINCED
2 TABLESPOONS MINCED
   PARSLEY
3 TABLESPOONS OLIVE OIL
1 TABLESPOON VINEGAR

☐ In a casserole, make a thin layer of onion, cover with half the meat, and season with salt and pepper. Add more onions, more meat, and seasoning, and finish with a layer of onions.

☐ In a bowl, mix the butter and flour together and dot the onions with the butter mixture.

☐ Cover and simmer over low heat for 30 minutes.

☐ In a bowl, mix the anchovies, garlic, parsley, oil, and vinegar. Sprinkle over the casserole and simmer 1 hour longer or until tender.

YIELDS 4 SERVINGS.

Boeuf en Casserole Provençale

Casserole of Beef with Tomatoes, Onions, and Olives

☐ Cut the meat into 1½-inch cubes. In a skillet, brown the meat in 2 tablespoons of butter. Remove the beef from the pan, add the Cognac, and ignite. Stir to loosen the browned bits.

☐ Add the remaining tablespoon of butter to the skillet, with the onion and garlic, and cook until lightly glazed. Add the tomatoes and olives and cook for 2 minutes.

☐ Add the tomato paste, potato flour, and meat glaze, off the heat, stirring until smooth.

☐ Add the wine, chicken stock, and sherry. Return to low heat and bring to a simmer.

☐ Stir in the jelly and tarragon, and return the beef to the pan. Cover and simmer over low heat until tender, about 1 hour.

☐ Serve sprinkled with the parsley.

YIELDS 6 SERVINGS.

INGREDIENTS:

2½ POUNDS EYE ROUND OF BEEF

3 TABLESPOONS BUTTER

2 TABLESPOONS COGNAC

3 ONIONS, CUT IN EIGHTHS

1 CLOVE GARLIC, MINCED

4 TOMATOES, PEELED AND CUT INTO EIGHTHS

½ CUP STUFFED OLIVES

2 TEASPOONS TOMATO PASTE

1 TEASPOON POTATO STARCH

1 TEASPOON MEAT GLAZE

½ CUP RED WINE

1 CUP CHICKEN STOCK

¼ CUP SHERRY

1 TEASPOON CURRANT JELLY

½ TEASPOON TARRAGON

2 TABLESPOONS MINCED PARSLEY

Shish Kebabs

☐ Cut the lamb into 2-inch cubes. Cut the tomato into 4 wedges. Cut the onion into 4 wedges. Cut the peppers into 1½-inch squares.

☐ In a bowl, combine the olive oil, lemon juice, oregano, salt, and pepper. Add the meat and vegetables and marinate for 1 hour. Drain and thread on skewers.

☐ Broil for 5 to 7 minutes or until the meat is browned on all sides. The meat should be medium rare.

YIELDS 4 SERVINGS.

INGREDIENTS:

½ POUND LAMB PER SERVING

1 TOMATO PER SERVING

1 ONION PER SERVING

1 GREEN PEPPER PER SERVING

½ CUP OLIVE OIL

¼ CUP LEMON JUICE

1 TEASPOON DRIED OREGANO

SALT AND PEPPER TO TASTE

Agneau Grillé au Thyme

Lamb Grilled with Thyme

INGREDIENTS:

2 LAMB STEAKS, 1-INCH THICK
1 CLOVE GARLIC
THYME
4 TABLESPOONS OLIVE OIL
3 TABLESPOONS BUTTER
SALT AND PEPPER TO TASTE

☐ Make a few slashes through the fat around the steaks to prevent them from curling. (Be sure to cut no deeper than the fat.)

☐ Cut the garlic clove in half and rub over the steaks.

☐ Sprinkle with thyme and press into the flesh. (As always, you can substitute other herbs for the thyme – try using oregano or savory.) Brush with olive oil. Broil 5 minutes on each side.

☐ Place on a platter and put a good-sized piece of butter on each steak. Season with salt and pepper.

YIELDS 2 TO 4 SERVINGS.

Turkish Lamb Skewers

INGREDIENTS:

1 POUND GROUND LAMB
SALT AND PEPPER TO TASTE
1 EGG, LIGHTLY BEATEN
1 SMALL ONION, GRATED
OLIVE OIL
1 TEASPOON PAPRIKA
¼ CUP YOGURT
1 CLOVE GARLIC, MINCED
4 SLICES HOT BUTTERED TOAST
3 TABLESPOONS HOT MELTED BUTTER

☐ In a bowl, combine the lamb, salt, pepper, and egg.

☐ Squeeze the onion through a coffee filter or kitchen towel to make 1 tablespoon of juice. Add the juice to the lamb.

☐ Divide the mixture into 4 portions and roll each into a sausage. Brush the rolls with oil and run a wooden skewer through the center of each.

☐ In a bowl, mix the yogurt and garlic, and season with salt and pepper.

☐ Grill, turning often, until the lamb is cooked.

☐ Arrange the rolls on buttered toast, spoon the sauce over each one, and pour on the melted butter. Sprinkle with paprika.

YIELDS 4 SERVINGS.

Brochettes d'Agneau aux Herbes de Provence
Broiled Herbed Lamb

☐ In a bowl, crush the thyme, rosemary, bay leaf, garlic, parsley, salt, and pepper. Stir in the olive oil. Transfer to a shallow dish.

☐ Toss the lamb, peppers, and onions in the marinade and let stand for 2 hours, turning often.

☐ Arrange the meat and vegetables on skewers and grill until the lamb is well browned on the outside but still pink in the center.

YIELDS 4 SERVINGS.

INGREDIENTS:
1 TEASPOON THYME
1 TEASPOON ROSEMARY
1 BAY LEAF
3 GARLIC CLOVES, CRUSHED
2 TABLESPOON MINCED PARSLEY
SALT AND PEPPER TO TASTE
⅓ CUP OLIVE OIL
1½ POUND LAMB, CUBED
2 RED PEPPERS, QUARTERED
2 ONIONS, QUARTERED

Farikol
Norwegian Lamb and Cabbage Stew

☐ Cut the lamb and cabbage into 1-inch cubes and arrange in layers in a deep casserole. Sprinkle each layer with a little salt and flour.

☐ Add 2 cups of water and the peppercorns. Simmer, covered, for 1½ hours over low heat, or cook in a 350°F oven.

☐ Sprinkle with minced parsley just before serving.

YIELDS 6 SERVINGS.

INGREDIENTS:
2 POUNDS STEWING LAMB
1 LARGE HEAD OF CABBAGE
3 TABLESPOON SALT
3 TABLESPOONS FLOUR
2 CUPS WATER
10 BLACK PEPPERCORNS
2 TABLESPOONS MINCED PARSLEY

Escalopes de Veau Chasseur
Veal Cutlets Hunter Style

INGREDIENTS:

6 VEAL CUTLETS

FLOUR SEASONED WITH SALT AND PEPPER

4 TABLESPOONS CLARIFIED BUTTER, SEE PAGE 178

½ POUND MUSHROOMS, SLICED

1 TABLESPOON MINCED SHALLOTS

½ CUP WHITE WINE

¼ CUP TOMATO PURÉE

1 TEASPOON BEEF EXTRACT

1 TABLESPOON MINCED PARSLEY

1 TEASPOON DRIED TARRAGON

□ Pound the veal cutlets to tenderize and flatten slightly. Dredge the cutlets in the seasoned flour.

□ In a large skillet, sauté the veal until golden in clarified butter. Remove to a platter and keep warm.

□ Add the mushrooms to the pan and cook 2 minutes. Add the shallots and wine and cook until liquid is reduced to ¼ cup.

□ Add the tomato purée and beef extract. Cook 1 minute, stirring up the browned bits.

□ Stir in the parsley and tarragon and pour over the meat.

YIELDS 6 SERVINGS.

Escalopes de Veau en Aillade
Veal Cutlets with Garlic Sauce

INGREDIENTS:

3 TABLESPOONS OLIVE OIL

4 VEAL CUTLETS

SALT AND PEPPER TO TASTE

1 POUND TOMATOES, PEELED, SEEDED, AND CHOPPED

½ CUP DRY BREAD CRUMBS

4 CLOVES GARLIC, MINCED

¼ CUP MINCED PARSLEY

□ In a large skillet, heat the oil over moderate heat. Season the veal with salt and pepper, and sauté until golden.

□ Add the tomatoes and cook until they have melted.

□ Stir in the bread crumbs, garlic, and parsley, and cook 8 minutes longer or until most of the oil has been absorbed and the tomatoes resemble a thick sauce.

YIELDS 4 SERVINGS.

Escalopes de Veau Dijonnaise

Veal Cutlets with Mustard Cream

☐ Flatten the veal cutlets.

☐ In a skillet, melt the butter and sauté the mushrooms until softened and the liquid has evaporated.

☐ Spoon a little of the mushrooms into the center of each cutlet and season with salt and pepper. Fold the ends of the cutlet over the mushroom mixture.

☐ In a large skillet, sauté the veal in clarified butter until both sides are golden. Transfer to a serving dish and keep warm.

☐ Add 2 tablespoons of Cognac to the skillet and ignite. Shake until the flames go out. Stir up the browned bits and pour over the veal.

☐ Add the mustard and cream to the skillet and beat with a whisk over high heat until the cream is reduced and thick. Correct seasoning with salt and pepper. Pour over the veal.

YIELDS 8 SERVINGS.

INGREDIENTS:

8 THIN VEAL CUTLETS

3 TABLESPOONS BUTTER

¾ POUND MUSHROOMS, MINCED

¼ CUP CLARIFIED BUTTER, SEE PAGE 178

2 TABLESPOONS COGNAC

1 CUP HEAVY CREAM

1 TABLESPOON DIJON MUSTARD

SALT AND PEPPER TO TASTE

Côtelettes de Veau à l'Orange
Veal Chops with Oranges

INGREDIENTS:

8 LOIN VEAL CHOPS

10 TABLESPOONS CLARIFIED
  BUTTER, SEE PAGE 178

8 SLICES CANADIAN BACON

2 LARGE ORANGES

2 TEASPOONS FLOUR

3 TABLESPOONS WATER

2 EGGS, BEATEN

½ CUP HEAVY CREAM

SALT AND PEPPER TO TASTE

☐ In a skillet, sauté the veal chops in 8 tablespoons of the clarified butter until golden and cooked through, about 7 minutes per side.

☐ In another skillet, sauté the bacon in 1 tablespoon of clarified butter until heated.

☐ Carefully peel the orange zest from the oranges, trying not to include any of the bitter white pith. Cut the zest into very thin strips. Blanch in boiling water for 4 minutes, drain, and rinse.

☐ Squeeze the juice from the oranges.

☐ When the chops are cooked, season with salt and pepper and place on a platter.

☐ Stir the flour into the skillet and then stir in the orange juice and 3 tablespoons of water.

☐ Add the blanched orange strips and simmer 5 minutes, stirring. Season to taste with salt and pepper. Remove from the heat.

☐ In a small bowl, beat the egg and cream together, whisk into the skillet, and heat gently until slightly thickened. Pour over the chops.

YIELDS 4 TO 8 SERVINGS.

Blanquette de Veau à l'Ancienne
Veal Stew

□ Cut the veal into 1½-inch cubes. Cover with water and parboil for 5 minutes. Drain and rinse under cold water.

□ Cover with 1 quart of water and bring to a boil. Add the carrots, onions, salt, garlic, leek, peppercorns, and bouquet garni. Simmer for 1 to 1½ hours.

□ Remove meat, carrots, and onions and arrange on a serving dish. Keep warm.

□ Reduce the liquid to 1⅓ cups. Strain.

□ Meanwhile, simmer the mushrooms in ½ cup water, with ½ teaspoon of salt and the lemon juice, for 1 minute. Let stand in the liquid.

□ In a saucepan, melt the butter and stir in the flour. Cook until the roux just starts to turn golden.

□ Gradually add the cooking liquor from the meat and mushrooms and bring to a boil, stirring. Simmer 15 minutes, stirring often.

□ Combine egg yolks and cream and stir into the sauce. Bring to the boiling point, but do not let boil. Add the mushrooms to the veal on the platter. Season and strain the sauce over the veal and vegetables.

INGREDIENTS:
2 POUNDS VEAL SHOULDER
3 MEDIUM CARROTS
12 TO 15 SMALL ONIONS
2 TEASPOONS SALT
1 CLOVE GARLIC
1 LEEK
6 PEPPERCORNS
BOUQUET GARNI OF CELERY, PARSLEY, BAY LEAF, AND A PINCH OF THYME
1 POUND MUSHROOMS
½ CUP WATER
½ TEASPOON SALT
JUICE OF 1 LEMON
2 TABLESPOONS FLOUR
2 TABLESPOONS BUTTER
2 EGG YOLKS
1 CUP HEAVY CREAM

YIELDS 6 SERVINGS.

Cotes de Veau Braisées à la Chartres

Braised Veal Chops with Cheese

INGREDIENTS:

6 VEAL CHOPS
SALT AND PEPPER TO TASTE
2 CUPS FRESH BREAD CRUMBS
1 CUP GRATED PARMESAN
    CHEESE
2 TABLESPOONS BUTTER
2 TABLESPOONS MINCED
    ONION
⅔ CUP DRY WHITE WINE
1 TABLESPOON CORNSTARCH
PARSLEY SPRIGS

☐ Season the chops with salt and pepper.

☐ In a bowl, combine the bread crumbs and cheese, and mix well. Cover each chop with the mixture, pressing to make a compact, round topping.

☐ In a shallow casserole, melt the butter and spread in the onion. Place the chops on top of the onions and sprinkle with a little melted butter. Add the wine and cover.

☐ Braise in a 400°F oven for 1½ hours or until the meat is very tender.

☐ During the cooking, add a little water at a time to keep the veal moist. Baste the chops with the juices as they collect. If the topping cracks, press it back together carefully but firmly. Transfer to a serving platter.

☐ Pour the juices into a saucepan and thicken with the cornstarch mixed with 1 tablespoon of cold water. Add only a little of the cornstarch at a time until the sauce is thickened to the desired consistency. You will probably not need all of the cornstarch mixture. Pour the juices around the chops and garnish with parsley sprigs.

YIELDS 6 SERVINGS.

Paupiettes de Veau avec Sauce Moutarde
Veal Birds with Mustard Sauce

☐ In a bowl, mix the sausage, garlic, half the onion, parsley, egg yolks, salt, and pepper.

☐ Divide this mixture into 8 parts and spread down the center of each cutlet. Roll and tie with a string.

☐ In a skillet, melt the butter and cook the veal, turning, until browned on all sides.

☐ Add the remaining onion, cover, and simmer gently until the veal is tender, about 30 minutes. Remove the veal to a platter and keep warm. Remove the string. Stir the mustard into the skillet, add the cream, and cook, stirring, until thickened, about 5 minutes. Spoon over the Veal Birds and serve.

YIELDS 8 SERVINGS.

INGREDIENTS:
1 POUND MILD SAUSAGE MEAT
1 GARLIC CLOVE, CRUSHED
2 ONIONS, MINCED
1 TABLESPOON MINCED PARSLEY
2 EGG YOLKS
1 TEASPOON SALT
½ TEASPOON PEPPER
8 LARGE VEAL CUTLETS, POUNDED
8 TABLESPOONS BUTTER
3 TABLESPOONS DIJON MUSTARD
1 CUP HEAVY CREAM

Côtelettes de Porc Charcutière
Pork Chops Charcuterie Style

☐ Sauté the pork chops in butter.

☐ Add the onions and sauté until golden.

☐ Add the wine and vinegar and reduce to ¼ of the volume.

☐ Add the tomato purée and simmer 10 minutes.

☐ Add the mustard and cornichons. Heat through and serve.

YIELDS 4 SERVINGS.

INGREDIENTS:
4 PORK CHOPS
1 TABLESPOON BUTTER
2 TABLESPOONS MINCED ONION
⅓ CUP WHITE WINE
1 TABLESPOON VINEGAR
1 CUP TOMATO PURÉE
1 TEASPOON MUSTARD
5 CORNICHONS, SLICED

Caribbean Pork Chops

INGREDIENTS:
4 PORK CHOPS
FLOUR
SALT AND PEPPER TO TASTE
4 TABLESPOONS BUTTER
1 LARGE ONION, SLICED
2 CLOVES GARLIC, MINCED
1 BAY LEAF
1 CINNAMON STICK
4 TOMATOES, SLICED
4 FIRM BANANAS
LEMON JUICE

☐ Preheat the oven to 300°F.

☐ Dredge the pork chops with flour seasoned with salt and pepper.

☐ In a skillet, brown the chops in 2 tablespoons of the butter until browned on both sides. Remove and reserve.

☐ Add the onion to the skillet and cook until golden. Add the garlic and cook 2 minutes longer, stirring constantly.

☐ Spread the onions evenly over the bottom of the skillet and top with the bay leaf, cinnamon stick, and chops.

☐ Cover the chops with tomato slices and season with salt and pepper. Seal and bake for 1 hour.

☐ Peel bananas and slice lengthwise. Flour lightly.

☐ In a large skillet, sauté the bananas until golden in the remaining 2 tablespoons of butter. Lightly toss with lemon juice. Arrange over the chops and serve.

YIELDS 4 SERVINGS.

Brochettes de Porc au Romarin
Rosemary Pork en Brochette

INGREDIENTS:
1¼ POUNDS LEAN PORK LOIN
2 TABLESPOONS OIL
1 TABLESPOON RED WINE VINEGAR
1 TEASPOON CHOPPED ROSEMARY
SALT AND PEPPER TO TASTE
1 CLOVE GARLIC, MINCED

☐ Cut the pork into 1-inch cubes and place in a bowl.

☐ Add the oil, vinegar, rosemary, salt, pepper, and garlic. Toss to combine and let marinate at least 1 hour, stirring occasionally.

☐ Arrange pork cubes on skewers and grill, turning often, for about 20 minutes or until cooked through.

YIELDS 4 TO 6 SERVINGS.

Côtes de Porc à la Flamande

☐ Preheat oven to 350°F.

☐ Season the chops with salt and pepper.

☐ In a skillet, sauté on both sides in the butter until half-cooked. Place in an ovenproof serving dish.

☐ Slice the apples and arrange on top of the chops.

☐ Baste with the butter from the skillet and bake for 25 minutes, or simmer over very low heat for 25 minutes until cooked through. Baste often with the butter.

INGREDIENTS:
6 PORK CHOPS
SALT AND PEPPER TO TASTE
3 TABLESPOONS BUTTER
3 BAKING APPLES, PEELED AND CORED

YIELDS 6 SERVINGS.

Medallions of Pork with Red Wine

☐ Pound chops to ⅓-inch thickness.

☐ In a large skillet, cook the chops in two batches over moderately high heat in 2 tablespoons of the butter for 2 minutes on each side. Remove and keep warm.

☐ Add the remaining tablespoon of butter and the shallots to the pan and sauté 1 minute.

☐ Add the beef stock and boil 1 minute, scraping up the browned bits. Add the wine, thyme, and sugar, and simmer 3 minutes. Arrange the chops on a platter, spoon the sauce over them, and sprinkle with chives.

INGREDIENTS:
8 BONELESS PORK CHOPS
3 TABLESPOONS BUTTER
2 SHALLOTS, MINCED
1 CUP BEEF STOCK
½ CUP RED WINE
½ TEASPOON THYME
½ TEASPOON SUGAR
2 TABLESPOONS MINCED CHIVES

YIELDS 8 SERVINGS.

Ragoût de Porc

Pork Stew Farmer Style

INGREDIENTS:

2-POUND PORK SHOULDER, CUT INTO 1-INCH CUBES

1 TEASPOON SALT

PEPPER TO TASTE

2 TABLESPOONS LARD

1 ONION, CHOPPED

1 CARROT, DICED

3 LEEKS, MINCED

1 CLOVE GARLIC, CRUSHED

2 TABLESPOONS FLOUR

½ CUP WATER

1½ CUPS CHOPPED CELERY

BOUQUET GARNI OF PARSLEY, BAY LEAF, AND THYME

6 POTATOES, PEELED AND CUT INTO CHUNKS

1 TEASPOON MINCED PARSLEY

☐ Season the pork with salt and pepper.

☐ In a large skillet, brown the pork in the lard and remove to a casserole.

☐ Add the onion, carrot, and leeks to the skillet and cook until they start to turn brown. Pour off any surplus fat.

☐ Add the flour and garlic and mix well. Cook a few minutes to brown the flour.

☐ Transfer the vegetables to the casserole and add ½ cup water to the skillet. Bring to a boil, stirring up the browned bits. Add the liquid to the casserole. Add just enough extra water to cover the pork. Bring to a boil and add the celery and bouquet garni. Cover and simmer slowly for about 25 minutes.

☐ Add the potatoes and cook for 40 minutes longer or until the meat is tender and the potatoes are cooked.

☐ Remove the bouquet garni and skim the fat from the top. Sprinkle with parsley and serve.

YIELDS 6 SERVINGS.

SEVEN

PASTA

I have never met anyone who did not like pasta in one form or another – meatballs and spaghetti, macaroni and cheese, angel hair with fresh caviar, kreplach, wontons, ravioli, bean thread noodles, etc. Everyone likes pasta, and virtually every country uses some type of noodle product if it produces wheat or rice. I love pasta not only for its taste, but because I can create so many outstanding dishes in such short order.

Many pasta dishes are easily suited to boat cookery. The problem is not which recipes to include, but how to limit the number. There are certain pasta dishes that are not suitable – lasagna, for example. It is too much work. You can achieve the same effect with stuffed shells, but even those, I think, require too much work for boat cookery. Certainly some of the great pasta timbales, or molds lined with thin sheets of pasta, filled with pasta, meat and vegetable mixtures are too elaborate for a boat. But once these are ruled out, the possibilities are endless.

I do not recommend making pasta yourself, especially on a boat. For one thing, it does not dry well in a humid atmosphere. For another, you can buy excellent domestic and imported pastas in a huge variety of shapes. The same sauce used on different shapes will have different tastes. The shapes hold the sauce differently and therefore the flavor changes. Of course, the sauces themselves can be varied *ad infinitum*.

Many cooks believe that tomato sauces must be cooked forever. In fact, most can be prepared in less than 30 minutes. Freshly peeled, seeded, and chopped tomatoes are perfect, but not always available on board – or on land, for that matter. However, there are many excellent brands of canned tomatoes that work just as well as or better than fresh. Drain off the excess liquid and cook over fairly high heat until the tomatoes reach the consistency of a sauce.

In the past people believed that spaghetti sauce meant tomato sauce. This is untrue. Over the last several years, people have become more aware of the tremendous variety of sauces for pasta: garlic and oil, cream and cheeses, and bacon and eggs are just a few of the fabulous tomato-less pasta sauces around.

Another misconception is that all pasta is served with grated cheese. This is not the case. I have included several recipes that do not feature cheese. If you are going to need grated cheese, bring a block of aged Parmesan and grate it as needed. Forget those canned grated cheeses – they make sawdust taste good. Parmesan keeps well and is easy to grate on a four-sided grater. Just grate gently in a light circular motion over the medium-sized holes. Do not bear down or force the cheese over the grater; just go at it gently so that the cheese will grate and your knuckles will not.

Many people make "their" tomato sauce and prepare it in large quantities to have on hand in the freezer. I find it so easy to make a quick tomato sauce that I have never done this. Why use up freezer space? However, if you do bring along a container of frozen sauce, it will help to keep food cold, and few sailors will object to a plain spaghetti dinner. You can make meatballs fresh or prepare and freeze them beforehand. If you freeze them in the sauce, everything is ready to go.

Not every pasta sauce has to be cooked. There are a couple of recipes that are perfect for warm weather cookery. The sauces act as marinades for the hot pasta, which is served immediately or at room temperature.

Although the recipes that follow often specify what shape of pasta to use, you can nearly always substitute whatever shape you happen to have on hand. Generally, a sauce-like mixture without bits of food in it is particularly suited to the long thin pastas, such as spaghetti, linguine, or vermicelli. If there is cubed food, such as tomatoes or meat, that would slide off the long shapes, it is better to use the more cupped shapes such as shells, gnocchi, cavatelli, or orecchiette. Light sauces generally go with more delicate shapes, and heartier sauces, with more substantial shapes. Therefore, a full-bodied tomato sauce would be better with rigatoni, penne, or elbows rather than angel hair. But within a given range, mix at will. If the recipe calls for spaghetti and you have vermicelli, use that. Substitute rigatoni for penne or even the corkscrew shapes.

NUMBER OF SERVINGS

The recipes indicate that a pound of pasta will serve six persons. This provides a reasonably substantial main course serving with a menu that might include a first course, salad, and dessert. Some diners feel that less than a quarter-pound of pasta per person is indecent; others would prefer to have the pasta as a first course, in which case a pound should serve eight easily. You have to decide what quantity you and your shipmates will consume.

Fettucine with Goat Cheese

You can use any one or a combination of the herbs. In addition to those listed, try rosemary or summer savory.

☐ In a saucepan, simmer the cream, goat cheese, and garlic until thickened and smooth, about 15 minutes, stirring constantly.

☐ Cook the pasta in boiling salted water until *al dente*. Drain.

☐ Toss the pasta with the sauce and sprinkle generously with the pepper and the herbs.

YIELDS 6 SERVINGS.

INGREDIENTS:

2 CUPS HEAVY CREAM

2 OUNCES GOAT CHEESE, RIND REMOVED AND CRUMBLED

2 CLOVES GARLIC, MINCED

1 POUND FETTUCINE OR OTHER FLAT PASTA

PEPPER TO TASTE

½ CUP PARSLEY, CHERVIL, AND/OR BASIL, MINCED

Spaghetti with Gorgonzola Sauce

Although Italian Gorgonzola is recommended, other blue cheeses can be substituted. In fact, this is a basic cheese sauce for pasta and you can use Gruyère, Fontina, or any other cheese you like.

☐ In a saucepan, heat the Gorgonzola, milk, butter, and salt, mashing the cheese. Simmer until the sauce reaches a dense, creamy consistency. Stir in the cream.

☐ Meanwhile, cook the pasta in boiling salted water until *al dente*. Drain.

☐ Toss the pasta with the sauce and sprinkle on the Parmesan. Toss again.

YIELDS 6 SERVINGS.

INGREDIENTS:

4 OUNCES GORGONZOLA

⅓ CUP MILK

3 TABLESPOONS BUTTER

SALT TO TASTE

¼ CUP HEAVY CREAM

1 POUND SPAGHETTI

⅓ CUP GRATED PARMESAN CHEESE

Elbow Macaroni, Greek Style

There are numerous small tubular pasta shapes that can be used for this recipe. The one you choose should be no longer than one inch. Cacciocavallo is a grating cheese that may not be readily available. Substitute Romano or Parmesan for it.

INGREDIENTS:
2 ONIONS, CHOPPED
¼ POUND BUTTER
1 POUND ELBOWS OR OTHER TUBULAR PASTA
1 PINT SOUR CREAM OR YOGURT
1½ CUPS CRUMBLED FETA CHEESE
12 KALAMATA OLIVES, SLICED
½ CUP GRATED CACCIOCAVALLO CHEESE
SALT AND PEPPER TO TASTE
1 POUND SPINACH, COOKED AND CHOPPED

☐ In a skillet, sauté the onions in the butter until they are very soft and just starting to turn golden.

☐ Cook the pasta in the boiling salted water until tender. Drain.

☐ In a bowl, mix the hot pasta, onion, sour cream, feta, olives, and grated cheese. Toss and season with salt and pepper.

☐ Add the spinach, toss again, and serve with additional feta cheese, if desired.

YIELDS 6 SERVINGS.

Penne coi Piselli e Peperoni
Penne with Peas and Peppers

To peel peppers, put them under a broiler until the skin is charred on all sides. Then put them in a paper bag, sealed, for 10 minutes. The skins will peel off. Frankly, this is perhaps more work than you want to do on a boat. You can buy roasted peppers in the Italian section of your market and use those or pimientos, which are the same thing.

INGREDIENTS:
3 RED PEPPERS, PEELED
1 SLICE OF PROSCIUTTO, ¼-INCH THICK
4 TABLESPOONS BUTTER
1 CUP TINY PEAS, COOKED
1 CUP HEAVY CREAM
SALT AND PEPPER TO TASTE
1 POUND PENNE
1 CUP GRATED PARMESAN

☐ Cut the peppers into ¼-inch squares.

☐ In a skillet, heat the prosciutto in the butter, add the peas, and cook 1 minute. Stir in the peppers, cream, salt, and pepper, and simmer, stirring, until the cream thickens.

☐ Cook the pasta in boiling salted water until *al dente*. Drain.

☐ Toss the pasta with the hot sauce and the cheese.

YIELDS 6 SERVINGS.

Linguine con Salsa Verde
Linguine with Green Sauce

☐ Strip the spinach leaves of their stems and cook in a kettle with only the water that remains on the leaves. Drain in a colander, run under cold water, and squeeze out excess moisture. (For frozen spinach, follow package directions.) Chop finely.

☐ Simmer the onions in boiling salted water for 20 minutes, drain, and chop finely.

☐ In a skillet, heat the oil and add the anchovies, onions, spinach, a little salt, and water. Simmer, stirring, for 5 minutes.

☐ Cook the pasta in boiling salted water until *al dente*. Drain.

☐ In a large bowl, toss the pasta with the sauce. Do not serve cheese with this sauce.

YIELDS 6 SERVINGS.

INGREDIENTS:
1 POUND SPINACH OR 10 OUNCES FROZEN
SALT TO TASTE
3 LARGE ONIONS, THINLY SLICED
2 TABLESPOONS OLIVE OIL
1 2-OUNCE CAN OF FLAT ANCHOVY FILLETS, DRAINED
3 TABLESPOONS WATER
1 POUND LINGUINE

Linguine con Peperoni Freschi
Linguine with Fresh Peppers

☐ In a skillet, sauté the onion in the oil until it starts to brown. Add the garlic and cook, stirring, for 1 minute.

☐ Cut the peppers into thin strips and add them to the onions along with the pepper flakes, tomato sauce, salt, and pepper. Cook, stirring, until hot. Stir in the parsley.

☐ Toss the cooked linguine with the sauce. The pasta can be served with grated Parmesan cheese.

YIELDS 6 SERVINGS.

INGREDIENTS:
¼ CUP OLIVE OIL
1 ONION, THINLY SLICED
1½ TEASPOONS MINCED GARLIC
4 RED OR GREEN PEPPERS, PEELED
¼ TEASPOON CRUSHED RED PEPPER FLAKES
1 CUP FRESH TOMATO SAUCE, SEE PAGE 117
SALT AND PEPPER TO TASTE
¼ POUND MINCED PARSLEY
1 POUND LINGUINE, COOKED

Spaghetti con Vongole

Spaghetti with Clam Sauce

A 10-ounce can of clams can be substituted for the fresh clams.

INGREDIENTS:
18 LITTLENECK CLAMS
½ CUP BUTTER
⅔ CUP MINCED ONION
2 TABLESPOONS OLIVE OIL
4 TEASPOONS FLOUR
½ CUP WHITE WINE
2 TABLESPOONS MINCED
  PARSLEY
SALT AND PEPPER TO TASTE
1 POUND SPAGHETTI

☐ Shuck the clams, reserving the juice, and mince them.

☐ In a skillet, sauté the onions in the butter and oil until lightly colored, sprinkle them with flour, and cook, stirring, for 3 minutes.

☐ Stir in the clam juice and wine, and cook, stirring, until thickened and smooth.

☐ Add the parsley and the clams. Season with salt and pepper. Be careful not to boil the sauce, or the clams will toughen.

☐ Cook the pasta in boiling salted water until tender. Drain. Toss with the sauce.

YIELDS 6 SERVINGS.

Vermicelli with Mushrooms and Marjoram

INGREDIENTS:
¼ POUND MUSHROOMS,
  THINLY SLICED
¼ CUP BUTTER
1 TEASPOON CRUSHED
  MARJORAM
2 TABLESPOONS MINCED
  PARSLEY
SALT AND PEPPER TO TASTE
½ POUND VERMICELLI

☐ In a saucepan, cook the mushrooms in the butter over low heat, stirring, for about 3 minutes. Sprinkle with marjoram, parsley, salt, and pepper.

☐ Cook the pasta in boiling salted water until *al dente*. Drain.

☐ Toss the hot pasta with the mushroom sauce and serve.

YIELDS 2 TO 3 SERVINGS.

Spaghetti with Mussels, Scallops, and Shrimp

You can vary the amounts of the shellfish according to what is available. Use only scallops or only shrimp, if necessary, or add some crab or lobster.

☐ In a saucepan, sauté the onion in the oil until golden. Add the garlic and sauté 30 seconds. Add the wine, basil, and marjoram and cook for 1 minute.

☐ Add the tomatoes, increase the heat, and boil for 5 minutes.

☐ Lower the heat to medium and add the mussels or clams. Cover and cook until the shells open.

☐ Add the scallops and shrimp and cook them for 2 to 3 minutes or until they are barely firm. Correct seasoning with salt and pepper.

☐ Cook the spaghetti in boiling salted water until *al dente*. Drain.

☐ Toss the pasta with the sauce and serve.

YIELDS 6 SERVINGS.

INGREDIENTS:

3 TABLESPOONS OLIVE OIL
1 LARGE ONION, MINCED
2 GARLIC CLOVES, MINCED
¼ CUP DRY WHITE WINE
1½ TABLESPOONS MINCED FRESH BASIL
1 TEASPOON DRIED MARJORAM
1½ CUPS DRAINED CANNED TOMATOES
1½ POUNDS MUSSELS, SCRUBBED, OR 2 POUNDS SMALL CLAMS
1 POUND SCALLOPS
1 POUND SHRIMP, BUTTERFLIED
SALT AND PEPPER TO TASTE
1 POUND SPAGHETTI

Fresh Tomato Sauce

This is the simplest form of tomato sauce. It can be used on its own or in combination with other ingredients. For the best consistency, use plum tomatoes. Put the sauce through a food mill, if you like.

☐ In a saucepan, cook the tomatoes in the butter or olive oil over high heat for about 15 minutes. The sauce should be somewhat pulpy. Season with salt and pepper.

YIELDS ABOUT 2 CUPS.

INGREDIENTS:

2 POUNDS TOMATOES, PEELED, SEEDED, AND CHOPPED
3 TABLESPOONS BUTTER OR OLIVE OIL
SALT AND PEPPER TO TASTE

Tagliatelle con Tonno e Piselli
Pasta with Tuna and Peas

Tagliatelle is a flat-shaped pasta similar to fettucine, but you can substitute any long pasta, or even shells.

INGREDIENTS:
6½-OUNCE CAN TUNA IN OIL
½ CUP OLIVE OIL
1 CUP PEAS, COOKED
3 TABLESPOONS PARSLEY, MINCED
1 POUND TAGLIATELLE
3 TABLESPOONS BUTTER
BLACK PEPPER TO TASTE

☐ Drain the tuna, and break it up in a saucepan with the oil. Simmer for 2 minutes.

☐ Add the peas and simmer for 1 minute. Stir in the parsley.

☐ Cook the pasta in boiling salted water until *al dente*. Drain.

☐ Toss the pasta with the butter and mix in the tuna sauce. Sprinkle with pepper and toss again.

YIELDS 6 SERVINGS.

Salsa di Tonno
Tuna Sauce for Pasta

You can use any shape of pasta with this sauce. Try different shapes to see how they affect the flavor.

INGREDIENTS:
1 SMALL ONION, MINCED
¼ CUP OLIVE OIL
1 CUP TOMATOES, PEELED, SEEDED, AND CHOPPED
3½-OUNCE CAN TUNA IN OLIVE OIL
SALT AND PEPPER TO TASTE
1 POUND PASTA

☐ In a saucepan, sauté the onion in the oil until golden, over low heat.

☐ Add the tomatoes and cook until the liquid is evaporated.

☐ Drain the tuna and add it to the pan, breaking it up with a fork. Season with salt and pepper, and simmer about 5 minutes.

☐ Cook the pasta in boiling salted water until *al dente*. Drain.

☐ Toss the pasta with the sauce.

YIELDS 6 SERVINGS.

Spaghetti alla Carbonara
Spaghetti with Bacon and Egg Sauce

Pancetta is unsmoked Italian bacon. If it is not available, substitute American bacon. Stir in a little cream to make a smoother sauce.

This wonderful dish demands to be served with plenty of freshly ground black pepper and must be served immediately. Any waiting and it will lose its creamy consistency.

□ In a skillet, sauté the pancetta in the oil until the pieces are crisp. Remove the pancetta from the skillet and keep warm.

□ In a bowl, beat the eggs with half the cheese and a generous amount of black pepper.

□ Cook the pasta in boiling salted water until tender. Drain.

□ Transfer the spaghetti to the skillet and toss it in the oil with the pancetta strips until heated.

□ Remove from the heat and pour on the egg mixture. Toss again and serve *immediately*.

□ Serve the remaining cheese separately.

YIELDS 6 SERVINGS.

INGREDIENTS:
⅓ POUND PANCETTA, DICED
1½ TABLESPOONS OLIVE OIL
4 EGGS, LIGHTLY BEATEN
BLACK PEPPER
1 CUP GRATED PARMESAN CHEESE
1 POUND SPAGHETTI

SPAGHETTI ALLA PUTTANESCA
Spaghetti Whore's Style

This dish is named for the "Femmes de Nuit." There are several versions of the sauce and several theories about the origin of the name. One version is that a restaurant in Milan on a street favored by the ladies made the sauce. Another is that the ladies, having very little time for cooking, could make the sauce quickly between clients. The essential point is that these sauces are delicious and quickly made.

Spaghetti alla Puttanesca I

INGREDIENTS:

½ CUP OLIVE OIL

3 CLOVES GARLIC

1 POUND TOMATOES, PEELED, SEEDED, AND CHOPPED

2 TABLESPOONS CAPERS, DRAINED

12 LARGE BLACK OLIVES, PITTED

1 HOT CHILI PEPPER

1 TEASPOON MINCED FRESH OREGANO

PEPPER TO TASTE

3 OUNCES ANCHOVIES

3 SPRIGS PARSLEY, MINCED

1½ POUNDS PASTA

SALT TO TASTE

☐ In a skillet, sauté 2 of the garlic cloves in oil until golden brown. Discard the garlic. Crush the remaining garlic clove and add it to the skillet, along with the tomatoes, capers, olives, and chili pepper, and simmer for 20 minutes, stirring occasionally.

☐ Add the oregano, using ½ teaspoon dried oregano if fresh is not available. Add the pepper, anchovies, and parsley. Simmer 2 minutes longer. Discard the chili pepper.

☐ Cook the pasta in boiling salted water until *al dente*. Drain.

☐ Toss the pasta with the sauce and serve.

YIELDS 8 SERVINGS.

Spaghetti alla Puttanesca II

INGREDIENTS:

1 POUND SWEET ITALIAN SAUSAGE, CUT INTO ½-INCH SLICES

7 TABLESPOONS OLIVE OIL

4 CLOVES GARLIC, QUARTERED

2 28-OUNCE CANS ITALIAN PLUM TOMATOES, DRAINED AND CHOPPED

2 CUPS PITTED BLACK OLIVES, HALVED

2 TABLESPOONS CAPERS

½ TEASPOON CRUSHED RED PEPPER FLAKES

1 CAN ANCHOVY FILLETS, DRAINED AND MINCED

½ CUP MINCED PARSLEY

2 TEASPOONS DRIED OREGANO LEAVES

SALT AND PEPPER TO TASTE

1 POUND SPAGHETTI

☐ In a skillet, sauté the sausage in 1 tablespoon of the oil until brown on all sides. Drain on paper toweling.

☐ Sauté the garlic in the remaining oil in the skillet until soft; remove, and discard.

☐ Add the tomatoes, olives, capers, and red pepper flakes. Cook, stirring, until most of the juices evaporate, about 10 minutes.

☐ Add the anchovies, parsley, oregano, and reserved sausage. Cook until thickened, about 10 minutes longer. Correct seasoning with salt and pepper.

☐ Cook the spaghetti in boiling salted water until *al dente*. Drain.

☐ Toss the pasta with the sauce and serve.

YIELDS 6 SERVINGS.

Pasta alla Puttanesca III

This is not a mistake — the sauce for this version is not cooked.

☐ In a bowl, mix the tomatoes, garlic, basil, olive oil, salt, and pepper. Refrigerate for about 2 hours.

☐ Cook the pasta in boiling salted water until tender. Drain and place in a bowl. Pour on the cold sauce and toss well.

YIELDS 6 SERVINGS.

INGREDIENTS:

1 POUND TOMATOES, CHOPPED

4 GARLIC CLOVES, CHOPPED

½ CUP (PACKED) BASIL LEAVES, CHOPPED

½ CUP OLIVE OIL

SALT AND PEPPER TO TASTE

1 POUND PASTA SHELLS, SNAILS, OR PENNE

Spaghetti alla Siciliana
Spagetti Sicilian Style

The olives for this and other recipes in this section should be the imported olives, in brine or oil, from Italy or Greece. Canned black olives, though convenient, are tasteless and their texture is wrong.

☐ Salt the eggplant and put it in a colander to drain for at least 30 minutes.

☐ In a skillet, sauté the garlic in the oil until golden. Discard.

☐ Add the tomatoes and the eggplant to the oil, and simmer for 20 minutes.

☐ Cut the roasted pepper into strips and add to the sauce.

☐ Stir in the anchovies, olives, capers, and basil. Cover and simmer 10 minutes longer.

☐ Cook the pasta in boiling salted water until tender. Drain.

☐ Toss the pasta with the sauce. (For another version of this sauce, try stirring in ¼ cup of grated Romano and ¼ cup of ricotta before tossing with the pasta.) Serve with the grated cheese.

YIELDS 6 SERVINGS.

INGREDIENTS:

1 SMALL EGGPLANT, CUT INTO ½-INCH CUBES

SALT AND PEPPER TO TASTE

2 CLOVES GARLIC, CRUSHED

½ CUP OLIVE OIL

6 TOMATOES, PEELED AND CHOPPED

2 ROASTED PEPPERS

4 ANCHOVY FILLETS, CHOPPED

½ CUP BLACK OLIVES, PITTED AND HALVED

4 TEASPOONS CAPERS

2 TO 3 SPRIGS OF BASIL, MINCED

1 POUND SPAGHETTI

GRATED ROMANO OR PARMESAN CHEESE

UNCOOKED SAUCES

Over the last several years these pasta recipes have become increasingly familiar to cooks in this country. They have long been a summer favorite with Italians. They are easily assembled and make cooking on a boat easy.

Pasta with Cold Tomato-Olive Sauce

INGREDIENTS:

1½ POUNDS TOMATOES, PEELED, SEEDED, AND CHOPPED

½ CUP OLIVE OIL

2 CLOVES GARLIC, THINLY SLICED

½ CUP OIL-CURED BLACK OLIVES, PITTED AND CHOPPED

SALT AND PEPPER TO TASTE

PINCH OF HOT PEPPER FLAKES

3 TABLESPOONS MINCED FRESH BASIL

1 POUND SPAGHETTI

☐ About 2 hours before serving, mix the tomatoes in a bowl with the oil, garlic, olives, salt and pepper, dried pepper flakes, and basil. Refrigerate.

☐ Cook the pasta in boiling salted water until *al dente*. Drain.

☐ Toss the pasta with the sauce and serve.

YIELDS 6 SERVINGS.

Pasta with Uncooked Mushroom Sauce

INGREDIENTS:

3 TABLESPOONS MINCED PARSLEY

½ POUND MUSHROOMS, CHOPPED

1 ONION, MINCED

½ CUP OLIVE OIL

1 CLOVE GARLIC, CRUSHED

1 TEASPOON SALT

¼ TEASPOON FRESHLY GROUND BLACK PEPPER

1 POUND ZITI OR RIGATONI

☐ About 2 hours before serving, mix together the parsley, mushrooms, onion, olive oil, garlic, salt, and pepper, and let stand.

☐ Cook the pasta in boiling salted water until *al dente*. Drain.

☐ Toss the pasta with the sauce. Correct the seasoning with salt and pepper to taste.

YIELDS 6 SERVINGS.

Pasta di Casamicciola

Pasta Donkey's House

This is also known as Pasta alla Primavera, or springtime pasta. The name "primavera" is given to a number of recipes, which range from the simplest sauces, such as the one below, to elaborate preparations with over a half a dozen different vegetables cooked individually and finally held together with tomato and cream sauces. This version is similar to Pasta alla Puttanesca III.

□ In a bowl, combine the tomatoes, olive oil, basil, and enough lemon juice to make the mixture slightly tart. Season with salt and pepper. Let stand for 20 minutes before serving.

□ Cook the pasta until *al dente*, drain, and add to the sauce. Toss and serve immediately. Grated Parmesan does not usually accompany this dish, but use it by all means, if you like.

INGREDIENTS:

1 POUND TOMATOES, PEELED, SEEDED, AND CHOPPED

½ CUP OLIVE OIL

1 TABLESPOON MINCED BASIL

LEMON JUICE

SALT AND PEPPER TO TASTE

1 POUND CUP-SHAPED PASTA, SUCH AS CAVATELLI

YIELDS 6 SERVINGS.

Pasta with Uncooked Tomato and Mozzarella Sauce

□ Cut the tomatoes into strips and place in a bowl with the olive oil, basil, oregano, salt and pepper, capers, and Parmesan cheese. Refrigerate for 2 hours. Add the mozzarella to the sauce.

□ Cook the pasta in boiling salted water until *al dente*. Drain.

□ Toss the pasta with the sauce and serve immediately.

Note: For a flavor variation, add 1 large fresh red pepper, diced.

INGREDIENTS:

1 POUND RIPE TOMATOES, PEELED AND SEEDED

½ CUP OLIVE OIL

¼ CUP BASIL, CHOPPED

1½ TEASPOONS OREGANO

SALT AND PEPPER TO TASTE

2 TABLESPOONS CAPERS, DRAINED

¼ CUP GRATED PARMESAN CHEESE

8 OUNCES MOZZARELLA, DICED

1 POUND PASTA

YIELDS 6 SERVINGS.

EIGHT

VEGETABLES

Vegetables can present problems for the galley gourmet. They require a certain amount of time spent in peeling, perhaps seeding, chopping, slicing, dicing, etc. But these things have to be done no matter where you are, and there is no way out of it. There are some tricks, though, to make your cooking time easier. If you take a few minutes to bring a large pot of salted water to a full rolling boil while preparing breakfast, you can blanch vegetables such as broccoli, green beans or cauliflower, drain them and rinse them under cold water. They will be ready to finish cooking at dinner time. Of course, I think it only fair that members of the crew help with the peeling and, if necessary, the chopping.

Canned vegetables are used too often on pleasure boats, more because people are afraid that fresh vegetables will not keep than for any other reason. However, unless you are at sea for an extended period, you should be able to buy what you need at any port. If your taste runs toward the more esoteric vegetables, you could run into some problems. You won't find asparagus in Maine in August. But you can get fresh corn, potatoes, onions, carrots, cauliflower, broccoli, string beans, peas, green peppers, and possibly red peppers. Eggplant, tomatoes, and squash of one sort or another will probably be available. Fresh spinach should be available, and even though it requires more work, it is better than any of the frozen varieties.

A few vegetables freeze particularly well and are close enough in quality to fresh that I see no reason not to buy them. Peas, corn, and winter squash are good examples. Green beans are not too bad, but asparagus, carrots, and cauliflower, for example, all suffer a change in texture.

As I said earlier, a good brand of canned beets will do as well as fresh and, considering the time it takes to cook them, makes the most sense to have on board. Canned corn is also acceptable if you find a good brand. Test a few brands to find those that come closest to fresh. Apart from beets and corn, most canned vegetables are atrocious.

Vegetables can be cooked in numerous ways. They can be boiled, broiled, grilled, sautéed, roasted, poached, or braised. The recipes here have been chosen because they are delicious and particularly well suited for boat cookery. As always, if a recipe works for one type of vegetable, say, zucchini, you can substitute similar vegetables, such as summer squash or eggplant, without a problem. Or simply gather a variety and mix them together.

Potatoes rank as one of the more versatile foods, almost on a par with pasta. There are any number of ways of preparing them, often in advance. My preference is for boiled potatoes tossed with a flavored butter or sautéed potatoes that can cook while I am preparing the rest of the meal. Mashed potatoes and roasted potatoes involve more effort than I care to make. Of course, if you are having steak, baked potatoes can be cooked on the same grill or placed, wrapped in foil, buried in the ashes. Roasted potatoes require an oven and a roast – not something I recommend on a boat.

Rice is a good standby that takes up little space and can be used to prepare wonderful side dishes within a short time. You can save leftover rice and mix it with vegetables for a quick casserole, adding meat or fish if desired. Use it in a stir fry, add it to a soup, or use it to stuff a vegetable. It is always wise to have some rice on board if for no other reason than to prevent your salt from sticking.

French Cut Green Beans with Sesame Seeds

□ Trim the ends of the beans, and cut lengthwise between the seams or use a bean cutter. (If you choose to use frozen beans instead of fresh, just cook the beans until tender crisp and proceed with the next step.) Place in a steamer over boiling water and cook until tender, 6 to 10 minutes.

□ In a bowl, combine the sesame oil, lime juice, soy sauce, and sugar.

□ Toss the beans with this dressing and sprinkle with sesame seeds. Toss again.

□ Serve hot as a side dish or cold as a salad.

YIELDS 6 SERVINGS.

INGREDIENTS:
1½ POUNDS GREEN BEANS
¼ CUP SESAME OIL
2 TABLESPOONS LIME JUICE
¾ TEASPOON SOY SAUCE
½ TEASPOON SUGAR
¼ CUP SESAME SEEDS, TOASTED

Skewered Vegetables

INGREDIENTS:

2 SMALL ZUCCHINI
2 SMALL SUMMER SQUASH
2 SMALL RED ONIONS,
  PEELED
¼ CUP OLIVE OIL
½ TEASPOON OREGANO
SALT AND PEPPER TO TASTE

☐ Trim the ends from the zucchini and squash and cut into thin rounds.

☐ Cut the onions into ¼-inch-thick slices, being careful to keep the rings together.

☐ Put the vegetables in a bowl. Add the oil, oregano, salt, and pepper, and turn gently to coat. Let marinate for at least 20 minutes.

☐ Skewer the vegetables on 10-inch skewers. Broil until tender but still crisp, turning often. Brush often with the marinade.

Note: You can vary the vegetables according to what is available – red and green peppers, cherry tomatoes, sections of corn on the cob, etc. The herb can also be changed according to what is available and what flavors you prefer. Try using rosemary, thyme, marjoram or basil.

YIELDS 4 SERVINGS.

Fasole Verde cu Smintana
Green Beans with Sour Cream

INGREDIENTS:

1 POUND GREEN BEANS,
  SLICED LENGTHWISE
2 TABLESPOONS BUTTER
PINCH OF DRIED FENNEL
  SEED, CRUSHED
PINCH OF DILL SEED,
  CRUSHED
1½ TEASPOONS MINCED
  CHIVE
1½ TEASPOONS MINCED
  PARSLEY
½ CUP SOUR CREAM

☐ Cook the beans in boiling salted water until tender, about 10 minutes. Drain them and put them in a saucepan.

☐ Add the butter, fennel seed, dill seed, chive, parsley, and sour cream. Heat very gently, without boiling, for 10 minutes.

YIELDS 4 SERVINGS.

Sautéed Green Beans and Potatoes

☐ In a saucepan, cook the potatoes in boiling salted water to cover for 3 minutes. Drain.

☐ In the same saucepan, cook the beans in boiling salted water for 8 minutes. Drain.

☐ In a large skillet, heat the butter and cook the potatoes and garlic over high heat, stirring often, until they start to brown. Lower the heat to moderate and season with salt and pepper. Cook, stirring as needed, for 8 minutes.

☐ Add the beans and cook, stirring, for 2 to 3 minutes.

☐ Discard the garlic and serve.

YIELDS 4 SERVINGS.

INGREDIENTS:

3 IDAHO POTATOES, CUT INTO ½-INCH CUBES

½ POUND GREEN BEANS, CUT INTO 1-INCH LENGTHS

SALT AND PEPPER TO TASTE

3 TABLESPOONS BUTTER

1 CLOVE GARLIC, DENTED

Haricots Verts à la Francaise
Green Beans French Style

☐ Cut the beans into 1-inch-long pieces.

☐ In a large, heavy saucepan, place the beans, onions, and lettuce. Add 6 tablespoons of the butter and the sugar. Season lightly with the salt.

☐ Add the water, stir well, and bring to a boil.

☐ Add the parsley and chervil. Simmer, covered, until beans are cooked, about 15 minutes.

☐ Add the remaining 2 tablespoons of butter and serve.

YIELDS 8 SERVINGS.

INGREDIENTS:

2 POUNDS GREEN BEANS

1 POUND TINY WHITE ONIONS, PEELED

2 HEADS BOSTON LETTUCE, SHREDDED

8 TABLESPOONS BUTTER

1 TABLESPOON SUGAR

SALT TO TASTE

1¾ CUP WATER

1 TABLESPOON MINCED PARSLEY

1 TEASPOON DRIED CHERVIL

Ratatouille

This is a wonderful dish to have on board. You can serve it as a hot or cold vegetable, or add a little vinegar and use it as a salad. Chop it finely and serve it with crackers as an hors d'oeuvre. Mix it into scrambled eggs when they are just done or fold it into an omelet. Ratatouille keeps for several days in a cool place.

However, you will need a large pan (a casserole will do) and a fair amount of time for chopping and cooking. You might prefer to make this dish at home and bring it with you. Freeze it in small containers so that you can thaw the quantity you need.

INGREDIENTS:

8 TABLESPOONS OLIVE OIL

2 LARGE ONIONS, SLICED

2 GREEN PEPPERS, DICED

2 SMALL EGGPLANTS, DICED

6 SMALL ZUCCHINI, CUT INTO ½-INCH SLICES

6 TOMATOES, PEELED, SEEDED, AND CHOPPED

SALT AND PEPPER

2 TABLESPOONS MINCED PARSLEY

PINCH OF MARJORAM

PINCH OF BASIL

1 CLOVE GARLIC, CRUSHED

☐ In a large skillet, sauté the onions in the oil until soft but now brown. Add the peppers and eggplants and cook 5 minutes, stirring often. Add the zucchini and tomatoes and simmer gently for 30 minutes.

☐ Season with salt and pepper and sprinkle with parsley. Stir in the marjoram, basil, and garlic. Simmer 10 to 15 minutes more.

☐ Serve hot or cold.

YIELDS 8 TO 10 SERVINGS.

Carottes Nouvelles à la Vichy
New Carrots Vichy Style

INGREDIENTS:

1 POUND CARROTS, THINLY SLICED

½ CUP BUTTER

1 TABLESPOON SUGAR

1 TEASPOON SALT

2 TABLESPOONS COGNAC

☐ In a saucepan over medium heat, cook the carrots, butter, sugar, and salt, stirring often, until the carrots begin to brown.

☐ Add the Cognac and bake in a 300°F oven for 30 minutes. The carrots should have absorbed most of the moisture.

YIELDS 4 TO 6 SERVINGS.

Carrots and Grapes

□ In a saucepan over medium heat, cook the carrots, butter, and sugar until they start to look glazed. Cover with water and simmer until tender. Drain.

□ In a saucepan, heat the grapes in the butter and fold in the carrots. (For an interesting contrast of colors, try using Emperor grapes or another variety of red grapes.)

□ Sprinkle with parsley and serve.

YIELDS 6 SERVINGS.

INGREDIENTS:

36 SMALL CARROTS, CUT INTO JULIENNE OR ROUNDS

2 TABLESPOONS BUTTER

½ TEASPOON SUGAR

WATER

1 CUP GRAPES, HALVED AND PEELED (OPTIONAL)

1 TABLESPOON BUTTER

2 TABLESPOONS MINCED PARSLEY

Cardamom Carrots

□ Steam the carrots until tender.

□ In a skillet, toss the carrots, orange peel, cardamom, and salt in the butter for 2 to 3 minutes until the carrots are hot.

YIELDS 6 TO 8 SERVINGS.

INGREDIENTS:

2 POUNDS CARROTS, THINLY SLICED

¼ CUP BUTTER

1½ TEASPOONS GRATED ORANGE PEEL

½ TEASPOON GROUND CARDAMOM

SALT TO TASTE

Kentucky Minted Carrots

□ In a saucepan, cook the carrots in the water and salt, covered, until most of the water has evaporated and the carrots are tender. Stir in the butter, pepper, and mint. Correct seasoning and serve.

YIELDS 4 SERVINGS.

INGREDIENTS:

1 POUND CARROTS, SLICED ¼-INCH THICK

1 CUP WATER

1 TEASPOON SALT

3 TABLESPOONS BUTTER

PEPPER

2 TABLESPOONS MINCED MINT

Carote al Burro e Formaggio
Carrots with Butter and Cheese

INGREDIENTS:

2 BUNCHES OF CARROTS, THINLY SLICED
5 TABLESPOONS BUTTER
SALT TO TASTE
¼ TEASPOON SUGAR
3 TABLESPOONS GRATED PARMESAN CHEESE

☐ In a large skillet, arrange the carrots in one or two layers. Add the butter and ¼ inch of water. Cook over medium heat, uncovered.

☐ When the liquid has evaporated, add the salt and sugar. Cook, stirring occasionally, until the carrots are caramelized. Taste, and if they are still not tender, add 2 to 3 tablespoons of water and cook until tender. When cooked, stir in the Parmesan cheese and serve.

YIELDS 6 SERVINGS.

Broccoli alla Siciliana

INGREDIENTS:

1 LARGE HEAD OF BROCCOLI
1 TABLESPOON OLIVE OIL
1 ONION, THINLY SLICED
¼ CUP PITTED BLACK OLIVES, SLICED
2 ANCHOVY FILLETS, CHOPPED
1 CUP RED WINE

☐ Preheat the oven to 350°F.

☐ Cut the broccoli into florets and set aside. Peel the broccoli stalks and cut lengthwise into thin slices.

☐ Pour the olive oil into a baking dish. Layer the onion, olives, anchovies, and broccoli, alternating.

☐ Pour the red wine over the top and bake for 30 minutes or until vegetables are tender but not soft. This dish can be prepared in a tightly covered pot on top of the stove over very low heat.

YIELDS 4 TO 6 SERVINGS.

Choufleur Polonaise
Cauliflower with Polonaise Sauce

This sauce also works well with broccoli.

☐ Cook the cauliflower in boiling salted water until just tender. Drain.

☐ In a skillet, cook the butter over medium heat until it is hazelnut brown, and stir in the bread crumbs, lemon juice, egg, and parsley. Season with salt and pepper and pour over the cauliflower.

YIELDS 4 TO 6 SERVINGS.

INGREDIENTS:

1 CAULIFLOWER, CUT INTO FLORETS
SALT
½ CUP BUTTER
½ CUP FRESH BREAD CRUMBS
JUICE OF ½ LEMON
¼ CUP MINCED HARD-COOKED EGG
¼ CUP MINCED PARSLEY
SALT AND PEPPER TO TASTE

Céleris au Beurre
Celery in Butter

☐ Remove and discard the tough outer stalks of celery. Scrub and cut the hearts into small pieces.

☐ Cook, covered in 1 inch of boiling salted water, until almost tender, 8 to 10 minutes. Drain.

☐ Return the celery to the pan with the butter. Cover and simmer over low heat for 3 to 4 minutes.

☐ Correct seasoning with salt and pepper.

INGREDIENTS:

1 TO 2 BUNCHES OF CELERY
6 TABLESPOONS BUTTER
SALT AND PEPPER TO TASTE

Note: For a flavor variation, add a generous pinch of curry to the celery with the butter.

YIELDS 4 TO 6 SERVINGS.

Céleris au Fromage Gratiné

INGREDIENTS:

1 RECIPE OF CELERY IN BUTTER

½ CUP GRATED GRUYÈRE CHEESE

6 TABLESPOONS BUTTER

4 TABLESPOONS BREAD CRUMBS

☐ Preheat the oven to 350°F.

☐ Butter a baking dish and arrange celery in layers. Sprinkle with the cheese. Dot with butter and sprinkle with bread crumbs.

☐ Bake for 15 minutes.

YIELDS 5 TO 6 SERVINGS.

Fresh Fried Corn

INGREDIENTS:

6 EARS OF CORN

4 TABLESPOONS BUTTER

¼ CUP MINCED ONION

¼ TEASPOON SALT

PINCH OF WHITE PEPPER

¾ CUP HEAVY CREAM

☐ Cut the kernels from the cobs.

☐ In a large skillet, sauté the corn and onion in the butter for 3 minutes. Season with the salt and pepper and sauté for 7 minutes, stirring often.

☐ Remove from the heat and stir in the cream.

YIELDS 4 SERVINGS.

Maïs et Poivrons au Cari
Corn and Peppers with Curry

INGREDIENTS:

3 EARS OF CORN

1 CUP CHOPPED ONION

2 TABLESPOONS BUTTER

3 RED OR GREEN PEPPERS, CHOPPED

SALT AND PEPPER TO TASTE

1 TABLESPOON CURRY POWDER

½ CUP HEAVY CREAM

☐ Cut the kernels from the cob and set aside.

☐ In a skillet, sauté the onion in the butter until soft. Add the peppers and season with salt and pepper. Cook for 2 minutes. Sprinkle in the curry powder and stir to blend. Cover and simmer for 5 minutes, stirring twice.

☐ Add the corn and cream, and cook, stirring, for 1 minute or until the corn is just cooked.

YIELDS 4 TO 6 SERVINGS.

Sautéed Cucumbers and Snow Peas

☐ Blanch the cucumber pieces in boiling salted water for 2 minutes. Drain.

☐ In a skillet, sauté the cucumbers and snow peas in the oil over high heat for 2 minutes, stirring constantly. Season with salt and pepper and toss with the herb of your choice.

Note: Leftovers can be used as a salad base. Just toss with a little vinaigrette.

YIELDS 4 TO 6 SERVINGS.

INGREDIENTS:

2 CUCUMBERS, PEELED, SEEDED, AND CUT INTO 1-INCH SECTIONS

1 POUND SNOW PEAS, STRINGED

2 TABLESPOONS OLIVE OIL

SALT AND PEPPER TO TASTE

1 TABLESPOON MINCED BASIL, TARRAGON, OR MINT

Eggplant, Zucchini, and Tomato Gratin

☐ Preheat the oven to 350°F.

☐ In a large skillet, sauté the eggplant in the olive oil until both sides are golden. Remove and drain on paper towels.

☐ Mix the cracker crumbs with the cheese and marjoram. Sprinkle 2 tablespoons of this mixture on the bottom of a large gratin pan.

☐ Arrange alternate slices of eggplant, tomato, and zucchini down the length of the dish.

☐ Season with salt and pepper and sprinkle with the remaining cracker mixture. Dot with butter and bake for 20 minutes. Serve hot or at room temperature. Brown under the broiler, if you so desire.

YIELDS 6 SERVINGS.

INGREDIENTS:

2 MEDIUM EGGPLANTS, SLICED ½-INCH THICK

½ CUP OLIVE OIL

½ CUP CRUSHED SODA CRACKERS

2 TABLESPOONS GRATED PARMESAN CHEESE

1 TEASPOON MINCED MARJORAM LEAVES

2 LARGE TOMATOES, PEELED AND SLICED

2 POUNDS ZUCCHINI, SLICED ¼-INCH THICK

¼ TEASPOON SALT

PEPPER TO TASTE

3 TABLESPOONS BUTTER

Aubergines à la Provençale
Eggplant Provencale Style

INGREDIENTS:

3 SMALL EGGPLANTS

SALT AND PEPPER TO TASTE

3½ POUNDS TOMATOES, PEELED, SEEDED, AND CHOPPED

5 TABLESPOONS OLIVE OIL

3 TABLESPOONS MINCED PARSLEY

2 GARLIC CLOVES, MINCED

☐ Trim the eggplants and cut lengthwise into ⅓-inch-thick slices. Score lightly and season with salt. Let drain for 30 minutes.

☐ In a skillet, cook the tomatoes in 2 tablespoons of the olive oil for 10 minutes or until the liquid has nearly evaporated.

☐ Add the parsley, garlic, and salt and pepper. Simmer 10 minutes longer or until the mixture resembles a sauce.

☐ Pat the eggplant slices dry on paper toweling.

☐ In another skillet, heat the remaining 3 tablespoons of oil and brown the eggplant on both sides. Add more oil if needed. Do not crowd the pan. Drain the eggplant on paper toweling.

Note: To cook eggplant without using huge quantities of oil, make sure the oil is very hot before adding the eggplant. Dusting the slices with flour will create a crust that will prevent the eggplant from taking up too much oil. If you prefer, preheat the oven to 400°F. Brush each slice of eggplant with oil and bake until golden.

☐ Arrange on a platter and nappe with the sauce. This dish is also very good at room temperature.

YIELDS 4 TO 6 SERVINGS.

Baked Onions

INGREDIENTS:

6 MEDIUM ONIONS, UNPEELED

☐ Wrap each onion in aluminum foil and place it in the bed of a charcoal broiler. Let bake for about 1 hour.

☐ Serve each guest an onion wrapped in foil and let him or her open it and peel the onion. Pass butter, salt, and pepper separately.

YIELDS 6 SERVINGS.

Baked Tomatoes and Eggplant

☐ Preheat the oven to 350°F.

☐ Butter a large casserole with 3 tablespoons of the butter and make layers of eggplant, tomatoes, and grated cheese, seasoned with salt and pepper. Keep layering, ending with the cheese.

☐ Sprinkle with bread crumbs and dot with the remaining butter. Bake for 1 hour.

☐ This dish can be prepared the day before and served at room temperature.

YIELDS 6 SERVINGS.

INGREDIENTS:

8 TABLESPOONS BUTTER

1 POUND EGGPLANT, PEELED AND SLICED

2 POUNDS TOMATOES, SLICED

1½ CUPS GRUYÈRE, GRATED

SALT AND PEPPER TO TASTE

4 TABLESPOONS FRESH BREAD CRUMBS

Laitues en Chiffonade
Braised Shredded Lettuce

☐ Wash the lettuce, discard any wilted leaves, and cut off stem end. Cut lettuce into fine shreds.

☐ In a saucepan, heat 3 tablespoons of the butter and add the lettuce.

☐ Season with salt and pepper and add the stock.

☐ Cover and simmer gently for 5 to 10 minutes, depending on the type of lettuce.

☐ Drain and put into serving dish. Dot with the remaining butter.

YIELDS 4 SERVINGS.

INGREDIENTS:

4 HEADS OF LETTUCE

5 TABLESPOONS BUTTER

SALT AND PEPPER TO TASTE

4 TABLESPOONS CHICKEN STOCK

Pois Mange-Tout aux Champignons

Snow Peas and Mushrooms French Style

INGREDIENTS:

2 ONIONS, MINCED

3 TABLESPOONS BUTTER

½ POUND MUSHROOMS, QUARTERED

1 POUND SNOW PEAS, STRINGED

½ CUP HEAVY CREAM (OPTIONAL)

PAPRIKA TO TASTE

SALT AND PEPPER TO TASTE

☐ Sauté the onions in the butter until soft. Add the mushrooms and cook, stirring, for 3 minutes. Add the snow peas and mix well.

☐ Stir in the cream and bring to a boil. Sprinkle with paprika, salt, and pepper to taste.

YIELDS 6 SERVINGS.

Petits Pois à la Francaise

Peas French Style

INGREDIENTS:

1 HEAD OF BOSTON LETTUCE

3 CUPS SHELLED PEAS

6 PARSLEY SPRIGS, TIED TOGETHER

½ TEASPOON SALT

6 TABLESPOONS BUTTER

½ CUP WATER

½ TEASPOON SUGAR

☐ Remove any wilted leaves from the lettuce and trim the stem. Rinse in lukewarm water to cover. Cut into 4 wedges and shred each wedge.

☐ In a saucepan, combine the lettuce, peas, parsley, salt, butter, water, and sugar, and bring to a boil. Toss lightly.

☐ Cover and simmer 20 minutes or until peas are tender and liquid has evaporated. Discard the parsley and serve.

YIELDS 6 SERVINGS.

Spinach with Parmesan Cheese

☐ Preheat the broiler.

☐ In a skillet over high heat, combine the oil, butter, garlic, salt, and cayenne pepper.

☐ Add the spinach and toss until it is well coated and the leaves are bright green in color. Add the pine nuts and toss again.

☐ Transfer to a baking dish, sprinkle with Parmesan and melted butter. Brown under the broiler.

YIELDS 6 SERVINGS.

INGREDIENTS:
3 TABLESPOONS OLIVE OIL
2 TABLESPOONS BUTTER
1 TEASPOON MINCED GARLIC
SALT TO TASTE
PINCH OF CAYENNE PEPPER
2 POUNDS SPINACH, WASHED AND STRIPPED OF STEMS
¼ CUP PINE NUTS
3 TABLESPOONS GRATED PARMESAN CHEESE
2 TABLESPOONS MELTED BUTTER

Summer Squash Sicilian Style

☐ In a skillet, sauté the squash in the oil and garlic until tender.

☐ Add the vinegar, sugar, salt, and mint and cook 3 minutes longer.

YIELDS 4 SERVINGS.

INGREDIENTS:
2 POUNDS SUMMER SQUASH, THINLY SLICED
2 TABLESPOONS OLIVE OIL
1 CLOVE GARLIC, MINCED
3 TABLESPOONS WINE VINEGAR
1 TEASPOON SUGAR
1 TEASPOON SALT
2 TEASPOONS MINCED MINT

Baked Summer Squash

☐ Preheat the oven to 350°F.

☐ Arrange the squash in a baking dish. Pour on the melted butter and season with salt, pepper, and oregano. Bake for 20 minutes.

YIELDS 4 SERVINGS.

INGREDIENTS:
2 POUNDS SUMMER SQUASH, THINLY SLICED
¼ CUP BUTTER, MELTED
SALT AND PEPPER TO TASTE
GENEROUS PINCH OF OREGANO

Burgundy Onion Rings

INGREDIENTS:
4 LARGE ONIONS, SLICED
  ¼-INCH THICK
3 TABLESPOONS BUTTER
2 WHOLE CLOVES
SALT AND PEPPER TO TASTE
1 CUP FULL-BODIED RED
  WINE

☐ Separate the onions into rings.

☐ In a skillet, sauté the onions in the butter until well coated.

☐ Add the cloves and season with salt and pepper. Sauté until golden.

☐ Add the wine, cover, and simmer for 15 minutes or until tender.

☐ Discard the cloves and cook, uncovered, until the wine is reduced to a glaze.

YIELDS 4 SERVINGS.

Pommes de Terre Robert
Potatoes Robert

INGREDIENTS:
1 POUND POTATOES
SALT AND PEPPER TO TASTE
6 TABLESPOONS BUTTER
2 EGGS
2 TABLESPOONS MINCED
  CHIVES
2 TABLESPOONS OLIVE OIL

☐ Preheat the oven to 375°F.

☐ Bake the potatoes for 45 minutes or until tender. (Although the recipe calls for baking the potatoes, it will work just as well if the potatoes are boiled in their jackets and then peeled.)

☐ Cut the potatoes in half and scoop out the centers. Discard the shells or save to serve as an hors d'oeuvre.

☐ In a bowl, combine the potato pulp with the salt and pepper and 3 tablespoons of the butter. Beat well.

☐ Beat in the eggs and chives.

☐ Heat the oil and the remaining 3 tablespoons of butter in a skillet and spread the potatoes over the bottom. Cook over low heat until crusty and golden on the bottom. Turn the potatoes and cook the other side until golden and crusty.

☐ Serve hot.

YIELDS 4 SERVINGS.

Pommes de Terre à la Hongroise
Hungarian Potatoes

☐ In a casserole, sauté the onions in the butter until soft and golden. Add the tomatoes and paprika, and mix well. Simmer 10 minutes.

☐ Add the potatoes, season with salt, and mix well.

☐ Add enough stock to barely cover the potatoes and simmer, covered, for 30 minutes or until just tender.

☐ Serve sprinkled with the parsley.

YIELDS 4 SERVINGS.

INGREDIENTS:
3 ONIONS, MINCED
4 TABLESPOONS BUTTER
2 TOMATOES, PEELED, SEEDED, AND CHOPPED
4 TEASPOONS PAPRIKA
2 POUNDS POTATOES, PEELED AND SLICED
SALT TO TASTE
3 CUPS BEEF STOCK
6 TABLESPOONS MINCED PARSLEY

Pommes de Terre à la Grecque
Greek-Style Potatoes

☐ Cut the potatoes into quarters lengthwise.

☐ Place them in a shallow casserole. Add the butter, half of the lemon juice, and the beef stock. Season with salt and pepper. Bake for 15 minutes.

☐ Turn the potatoes and bake 15 minutes longer.

☐ Remove any excess fat from the dish and add the remaining lemon juice. Bake 5 minutes longer or until tender.

☐ Serve the potatoes sprinkled with minced parsley and lemon peel, which have been mixed together.

YIELDS 6 SERVINGS.

INGREDIENTS:
6 MEDIUM POTATOES, PEELED
⅓ CUP BUTTER
JUICE OF ½ LEMON
½ CUP BEEF STOCK
SALT AND PEPPER TO TASTE
MINCED PARSLEY
LEMON PEEL

Röesti, Fried Potato Cake

INGREDIENTS:

6 MEDIUM BAKING POTATOES

8 TABLESPOONS BUTTER, MELTED

SALT AND PEPPER TO TASTE

☐ Cook the potatoes for 5 minutes in boiling water to cover by 2 inches, drain, and peel.

☐ Grate the potatoes on the large holes of a grater.

☐ In a skillet, melt 2 tablespoons of the butter. Add a 1-inch layer of potatoes, spread evenly. Sprinkle with salt and pepper and drizzle with 1 tablespoon of butter.

☐ Continue layering until you have used all of the potatoes and butter. The mixture should be ½-inch above the pan.

☐ Place over moderate heat. When the butter begins to sizzle, cover the pan and press down on the lid. Cook, covered, 5 minutes.

☐ Remove the cover and shake the pan to make sure the cake has not begun to stick.

☐ Cook about 20 minutes or until the potatoes are a deep golden color.

☐ Turn the potato cake out onto a plate. Return it, now upside down, to the pan and quickly brown the bottom side, adding more butter if needed.

YIELDS 4 TO 6 SERVINGS.

Pommes de Terre à l'Ail

Garlic Potatoes

INGREDIENTS:

4 TABLESPOONS WALNUT OIL

2 POUNDS POTATOES, THICKLY SLICED

SALT AND PEPPER TO TASTE

GRATED NUTMEG TO TASTE

4 GARLIC CLOVES, CRUSHED

¼ CUP MINCED PARSLEY

¼ CUP MINCED CHIVES

☐ In a skillet, heat the oil, add the potatoes, and cook slowly. Season with salt, pepper, and nutmeg.

☐ Cook, stirring occasionally, for about 35 minutes or until potatoes are crisp, golden, and tender.

☐ In a bowl, mix the garlic, parsley, and chives. Stir into the potatoes and cook for 1 minute. Serve.

YIELDS 4 SERVINGS.

Sautéed Sweet Peppers and Zucchini

□ In a large skillet, sauté the onion and pepper in the oil until slightly softened.

□ Add the zucchini, garlic, and herbs and stir fry another 2 minutes or until the vegetables are just tender.

□ Correct seasoning with salt and pepper.

YIELDS 4 SERVINGS.

INGREDIENTS:
1 ONION, CUT INTO JULIENNE
1 RED PEPPER, CUT INTO JULIENNE
4 TABLESPOONS OLIVE OIL
2 ZUCCHINI, CUT INTO JULIENNE
1 CLOVE GARLIC, MINCED
¼ TEASPOON MINCED THYME
2½ TABLESPOONS MINCED BASIL
SALT AND PEPPER TO TASTE

Curried Rice with Mushrooms

□ In a large skillet, sauté the garlic in ¼ cup of butter until brown. Discard the garlic.

□ Stir in the mushrooms and cook until tender. Season with salt and pepper.

□ In a bowl, combine the rice, butter, curry powder, nutmeg, and onion. Toss lightly and fold in the mushrooms. Mix well.

□ In a 1½-quart casserole, spread a layer of tomato slices and cover with some of the rice mixture. Continue to make layers, ending with the rice.

□ In a small bowl, combine the bread crumbs and cheese and mix well. Sprinkle over the rice and dot with the 2 tablespoons of butter.

□ Bake at 350°F for 40 minutes or until heated through. Or assemble the casserole, set it over low heat on top of the stove, and cook until heated through. The topping will not brown, but it will taste wonderful.

YIELDS 6 TO 8 SERVINGS.

INGREDIENTS:
1 GARLIC CLOVE
¼ CUP BUTTER
1 POUND MUSHROOMS, THINLY SLICED
SALT AND PEPPER TO TASTE
2½ CUPS COOKED RICE
3 TABLESPOONS BUTTER
¾ TEASPOON CURRY POWDER
PINCH OF NUTMEG
¼ CUP MINCED RAW ONION
5 MEDIUM TOMATOES, SLICED
½ CUP FRESH BREAD CRUMBS
½ CUP GRATED PARMESAN CHEESE
2 TABLESPOONS BUTTER

Rice with Tomatoes

INGREDIENTS:

⅓ CUP MINCED ONION

½ TEASPOON MINCED GARLIC

2 TOMATOES, PEELED,
  SEEDED, AND CHOPPED

2 TABLESPOONS BUTTER

1 CUP RICE

1¼ CUPS WATER

1 BAY LEAF

SALT AND PEPPER TO TASTE

☐ In a saucepan, sauté the onion and garlic until soft, but not browned, in 1 tablespoon of the butter. Add the tomatoes and stir.

☐ Add the rice and stir until coated with the butter.

☐ Add the water, bay leaf, salt, and pepper and simmer, covered, for 17 minutes.

☐ Discard the bay leaf and stir in the remaining tablespoon of butter.

YIELDS 4 SERVINGS.

Riz à la Grecque
Rice Greek Style

INGREDIENTS:

2 TABLESPOONS BUTTER

1 ONION, MINCED

1 CLOVE GARLIC, MINCED

4 LETTUCE LEAVES,
  SHREDDED

4 MUSHROOMS, SLICED

4 TOMATOES, PEELED,
  SEEDED, AND CHOPPED

3 SAUSAGES, PEELED AND
  MASHED

1½ CUPS RICE

3 CUPS BOILING WATER

SALT AND PEPPER TO TASTE

1 TABLESPOON BUTTER

¾ CUP COOKED PEAS

1 PIMIENTO, DICED

☐ Preheat the oven to 400°F.

☐ In a saucepan with an ovenproof handle, sauté the onion in the butter until soft but not brown. Add the garlic, lettuce, mushrooms, tomatoes, and sausages. Stir in the rice and mix well.

☐ Add the water, salt, and pepper and bring to a boil.

☐ Cover and bake for 20 to 25 minutes or until the rice is done.

☐ Fold in the butter, peas, and pimiento.

☐ As an alternative, the rice can be cooked on top of the stove. Cover, lower the heat to a bare simmer, and cook for 17 minutes. When the rice is done, toss everything lightly and add the butter, peas, and pimiento. Re-cover and let stand 5 minutes before serving.

YIELDS 6 SERVINGS.

Riz à la Basquaise
Rice Basque Style

□ In a saucepan, toss the rice with the butter and the 2 tablespoons of olive oil until it is well coated and lightly colored.

□ Add 1 cup of the stock, cover, and cook slowly until the liquid is absorbed.

□ Gradually add the remaining stock, cover, and cook until the liquid is absorbed.

□ In a skillet, sauté the pepper and onion in the ¼ cup of olive oil until they are soft but not brown. Season with salt and pepper, and mix them into the cooked rice, tossing with a fork.

YIELDS 4 SERVINGS.

INGREDIENTS:

1 CUP RICE

2 TABLESPOONS BUTTER

2 TABLESPOONS OLIVE OIL

2½ CUPS HOT CHICKEN STOCK

1 RED PEPPER, DICED

1 ONION, DICED

¼ CUP OLIVE OIL

SALT AND PEPPER TO TASTE

Zucchini with Herbs

□ In a skillet, sauté the zucchini in the oil over high heat for 5 minutes.

□ Season with salt and pepper. Drain off any excess oil.

□ Add the butter to the skillet and stir in the garlic, chives, dill, tarragon, and basil. Correct seasoning with salt and pepper.

YIELDS 6 SERVINGS.

INGREDIENTS:

1½ POUNDS SMALL ZUCCHINI, SLICED

4 TABLESPOONS OLIVE OIL

SALT AND PEPPER TO TASTE

2 TABLESPOONS BUTTER

2 TEASPOONS MINCED GARLIC

1 TABLESPOON MINCED CHIVES

1 TABLESPOON MINCED DILL

1 TEASPOON MINCED TARRAGON

1 TABLESPOON MINCED BASIL

Broiled Tomato Slices

INGREDIENTS:
3 LARGE TOMATOES
¼ CUP OLIVE OIL
2 TABLESPOONS MINCED
  BASIL
SALT AND PEPPER TO TASTE

☐ Cut the tomatoes into ½-inch slices and place in a baking dish. In a bowl, mix the olive oil, basil, salt, and pepper. Brush over the tomatoes and let stand for 10 minutes.

☐ Broil under a broiler or over charcoal for about 5 minutes.

YIELDS 4 SERVINGS.

Zucchini with Parmesan Cheese

INGREDIENTS:
6 SMALL ZUCCHINI
¾ CUP BREAD CRUMBS
¼ CUP GRATED PARMESAN
¼ CUP BUTTER
SALT AND PEPPER TO TASTE
1 TABLESPOON MINCED
  ONION

☐ Preheat the oven to 350°F.

☐ Slice the zucchini in half lengthwise. Make diagonal slashes into the flesh, but do not pierce the skin. Arrange in one layer in a baking dish.

☐ In a small bowl, combine the bread crumbs, Parmesan cheese, butter, salt, pepper, and onion. Spread on the cut side of the zucchini, pressing it into the slashes. Bake for 20 minutes.

YIELDS 4 TO 6 SERVINGS.

Zucchini and Carrots Julienne

INGREDIENTS:
6 ZUCCHINI, CUT INTO
  JULIENNE
2 TABLESPOONS BUTTER
2 TABLESPOONS OIL
6 CARROTS, CUT INTO
  JULIENNE
SALT AND PEPPER TO TASTE

☐ In a large skillet, sauté the zucchini and carrots in the butter and oil until they are tender but still crisp.

☐ Season with salt and pepper and serve hot or cold.

☐ Vary the flavor by adding garlic; an herb such as tarragon, dill, or chives; or a spice such as nutmeg, poppyseeds, or curry powder.

YIELDS 6 SERVINGS.

Zucchini with Cream

- ☐ Place the zucchini in a colander and sprinkle with the salt. Toss to coat and let stand for 20 minutes.

- ☐ Squeeze the zucchini in the corner of a kitchen towel.

- ☐ In a skillet, sauté the zucchini in butter and oil until tender, about 4 minutes.

- ☐ Season with pepper and nutmeg. Add the cream and herbs and bring just to a simmer.

YIELDS 4 SERVINGS.

INGREDIENTS:

1½ POUNDS SMALL ZUCCHINI, THINLY SLICED

2 TABLESPOONS SALT

¼ CUP BUTTER

2 TABLESPOONS OLIVE OIL

PEPPER TO TASTE

PINCH OF NUTMEG

3 TABLESPOONS HEAVY CREAM

2 TABLESPOONS MINCED BASIL OR CHERVIL

Courgettes à la Milanaise
Zucchini Milan Style

- ☐ Cut the zucchini into ½-inch-thick slices.

- ☐ Sprinkle the slices with salt and let them drain in a colander for 20 minutes. Dry the pieces on paper toweling, and dredge them in flour seasoned with salt and pepper.

- ☐ Sauté the zucchini in the olive oil until golden and tender.

- ☐ Place in an ovenproof baking dish. Sprinkle with melted butter and Parmesan cheese. Bake at 350°F for 10 minutes or until hot. (You do not have to bake the zucchini if they are hot when the butter and cheese are added.)

- ☐ Garnish with parsley.

YIELDS 6 SERVINGS.

INGREDIENTS:

2 POUNDS ZUCCHINI, SCRAPED

SALT AND PEPPER TO TASTE

FLOUR

OLIVE OIL

2 TABLESPOONS BUTTER

2 TABLESPOONS GRATED PARMESAN

1 TABLESPOON MINCED PARSLEY

Courgettes Farcies à la Variose

Stuffed Zucchini Provençale

INGREDIENTS:

4 ZUCCHINI

1 ONION, MINCED

2 TABLESPOONS OLIVE OIL

1 GARLIC CLOVE, MINCED

SALT AND PEPPER TO TASTE

1 TOMATO, PEELED, SEEDED, AND CHOPPED

2 TABLESPOONS MINCED PARSLEY

⅓ CUP RICE, BOILED FOR 18 MINUTES, RINSED, AND DRAINED

¾ CUP GRATED PARMESAN CHEESE

2 OUNCES STALE BREAD, SOAKED IN WARM WATER AND SQUEEZED DRY

¼ CUP OLIVE OIL

☐ Preheat the oven to 400°F.

☐ Trim the ends of the zucchini, cut in half lengthwise, remove the flesh, and mince. Reserve the shells.

☐ In a skillet, sauté the onion in the oil until soft but not brown. Add the chopped zucchini, garlic, and salt to taste. Cook over high heat for 10 minutes.

☐ Add the tomato and cook 10 minutes longer or until the liquid has evaporated, stirring occasionally.

☐ In a bowl, mix the parsley, rice, salt, pepper, half the Parmesan, and the cooked zucchini mixture.

☐ Rub the zucchini shells inside and out with olive oil and arrange in a baking dish. Spoon the filling into the shells, mounding with your fingers.

☐ Spread a layer of bread over the stuffed zucchini and press gently into place.

☐ Sprinkle with the remaining Parmesan and drizzle with the ¼ cup of olive oil.

☐ Bake for 45 minutes or until tender. This dish can be cooked on the top of the stove in a covered skillet, over low heat, until the zucchini are tender. Serve hot or cold.

YIELDS 4 TO 8 SERVINGS.

NINE

SALADS

Lettuce and other fragile ingredients need the same careful handling as other vegetables do on a boat. You can buy the sturdier lettuces such as romaine, iceberg, escarole, chicory, and the like, but many people prefer the more delicate Boston, Bibb, or red leaf. These should be bought for immediate consumption only. They will keep a day or two, depending on the refrigeration. Romaine, iceberg, chicory, and escarole will keep in an ice chest for several days. They have more body and are less likely to go limp in warm weather. There are people who despise iceberg lettuce, claiming that it is flavorless and hardly fit for human consumption. To each his own. I like the crunchy moistness of iceberg and when sailing, I like the fact that it keeps. Shred it to make a base for other salad mixtures, toss it in a salad with other greens, or use it in place of bread for a sandwich. Just spread the filling on the lettuce and roll it up like a crêpe. It is delicious and cuts down on the calories. It is *the* lettuce for a bacon, lettuce, and tomato sandwich.

It is not clear what constitutes a salad. You can make an attractive salad platter with both fresh food and leftovers. For example, place a bed of shredded lettuce on a platter. (Large leaves are too awkward to eat, especially if you are sitting on deck.) Mound some leftover rice that has been tossed with vinaigrette in the center. Surround the rice with some marinated string beans or some canned beets that have been coated lightly with mayonnaise or sour cream, mixed with a generous amount of mustard. Make a border of sliced tomatoes. Place mounds of diced chicken, fish, ham, or other meat at either end, garnish with hard-cooked eggs cut into wedges and a few black olives. Serve with additional vinaigrette or herbed mayonnaise. Lunch is served.

Often when I refer to leftovers, I mean not only the remains of an earlier meal, but also food that has been purposely cooked in extra-large quantities. If you are cooking string beans for four people, cook enough for six or eight so that you have enough to serve the next day at lunch or to pickle as an hors d'oeuvre. The object is to think ahead to the next meal. The people who simply refuse to plan ahead are the same people who all too often end up opening a can of beans. Not the person for whom this book is written.

There are all sorts of salads to prepare for family and guests. Consider the suggestions made here and realize that you can always make substitutions. Our recipe for cheese salad calls for Gruyère, cucumbers, and sweet red peppers, as well as croutons. If all you can get is cheddar and green peppers, go ahead. It won't be the same, but it will taste good.

MAYONNAISE

Good mayonnaise is vital not only to many salads, but also to sandwiches and hors d'oeuvres. I have never found a good commercial mayonnaise. Make your own. It is easier and much safer than you think. You can prepare a cup or two before you sail or make it on board. *You* control the flavor, making it more or less tart to suit your tastes. Homemade mayonnaise will last at least a week if it is kept in an icebox.

Many people mistakenly think that mayonnaise is unsafe in warm weather — that it causes bacteria to develop and leads to stomach problems. In fact, the food to which it is added is usually the problem, not the mayonnaise, whose acid helps preserve it. If the chicken or fish to which the mayonnaise is added is not fresh or has been allowed to sit out too long, it can develop bacteria that will make you ill — not the mayonnaise. So make your own and enjoy the best salads. For a good, basic recipe, see page 178.

Asparagus in Mustard Dressing

☐ In a bowl, mix the mayonnaise with the mustard. Add more if desired. Fold in the capers and season to taste with salt and pepper.

☐ Arrange the asparagus on a platter and coat with the mustard dressing, leaving the tips exposed.

☐ Sprinkle with the minced parsley or pimiento, if desired.

YIELDS 4 TO 6 SERVINGS.

INGREDIENTS:

¾ CUP MAYONNAISE, SEE PAGE 178

1½ TEASPOONS DIJON MUSTARD

2 TEASPOONS CAPERS, DRAINED

SALT AND PEPPER TO TASTE

2 POUNDS ASPARAGUS, COOKED

1 TABLESPOON MINCED PARSLEY OR PIMIENTO

Bean and Shrimp Salad

☐ In a bowl, mix the olive oil, lemon juice, salt, and pepper.

☐ Pour half the mixture over the beans and allow to cool.

☐ Pour the remaining half over the shrimp and allow to cool.

☐ Arrange the beans in a serving dish and garnish with the shrimp.

YIELDS 4 SERVINGS.

INGREDIENTS:

½ CUP OLIVE OIL

2 TABLESPOONS LEMON JUICE

SALT AND PEPPER TO TASTE

½ POUND GREEN BEANS, COOKED

½ POUND SHRIMP, COOKED AND PEELED

Beans Primavera

INGREDIENTS:

1 CAN (11 OUNCES)
CANNELONI BEANS

1 CLOVE GARLIC, MINCED

1 TABLESPOON MINCED
PARSLEY

1 TABLESPOON MINCED
FRESH BASIL

¼ CUP OLIVE OIL

1 TO 2 TABLESPOONS WINE
VINEGAR

SALT AND PEPPER TO TASTE

6 TOMATOES

☐ Drain the beans in a sieve, run under cold water, and drain again.

☐ In a bowl, mix the beans with the garlic, parsley, basil, olive oil, vinegar, salt, and pepper. Let stand for several hours.

☐ Cut off the stems of the tomatoes and scoop out the pulp and seeds. Discard the seeds.

☐ Mince the tomato pulp, fold it into the beans, and stuff the tomatoes with the mixture.

YIELDS 6 SERVINGS.

Green Bean Salad

INGREDIENTS:

1 POUND GREEN BEANS,
TRIMMED

3 TABLESPOONS RED WINE
VINEGAR

½ TEASPOON DRY MUSTARD

SALT AND PEPPER TO TASTE

½ CUP OLIVE OIL

8 TO 12 CHERRY TOMATOES

½ CUP THINLY SLICED
RED ONION

☐ Cook the beans in boiling salted water until tender crisp, drain, and rinse under cold water. Drain again.

☐ In a small bowl, beat together the vinegar, mustard, salt, and pepper, and slowly whisk in the oil until the mixture emulsifies and becomes smooth.

☐ Pour the dressing over the beans, add the tomatoes and onions, and toss gently. Let marinate for at least 1 hour.

YIELDS 4 TO 6 SERVINGS.

Broccoli with Sesame Dressing

☐ Season the broccoli with salt and pepper.

☐ In a bowl, combine the oil, vinegar, soy sauce, sugar, and pepper flakes. Mix well and toss with the broccoli. Sprinkle with the sesame seeds.

YIELDS 4 TO 6 SERVINGS.

INGREDIENTS:
1 BUNCH BROCCOLI, COOKED
SALT AND PEPPER TO TASTE
½ CUP SESAME OIL
¼ CUP RICE VINEGAR
1 TABLESPOON SOY SAUCE
½ TEASPOON SUGAR
PINCH OF RED PEPPER FLAKES
1 TABLESPOON SESAME SEEDS, TOASTED

Broccoli with Lemon and Garlic

☐ Cut the broccoli florets from the stems. Peel and slice the stalks. Cook the slices in boiling salted water for 2 minutes, add the florets, and cook until tender crisp. Drain, rinse under cold water, and drain again.

☐ In a bowl, mix the vinaigrette, lemon rind, and garlic slivers. Add the broccoli and toss gently. Let marinate for at least 1 hour.

YIELDS 4 TO 6 SERVINGS.

INGREDIENTS:
1 BUNCH OF BROCCOLI
½ CUP VINAIGRETTE, SEE PAGE 178
1 TEASPOON GRATED LEMON RIND
1 LARGE CLOVE GARLIC, CUT INTO SLIVERS

Carottes Râpées

☐ In a bowl mix the carrots and vinaigrette.

YIELDS 4 TO 6 SERVINGS.

INGREDIENTS:
1 POUND CARROTS, GRATED
¾ CUP VINAIGRETTE, SEE PAGE 178

Corn and Lima Bean Salad

Fresh coriander has a musky flavor that is not always appreciated. It is not always available and goes limp quickly. However, this salad works well with parsley, or you might try a large pinch of ground coriander.

INGREDIENTS:

6 EARS CORN, COOKED

1 10-OUNCE PACKAGE FROZEN LIMA BEANS, COOKED

½ CUP MINCED CORIANDER OR PARSLEY

LARGE PINCH OF CAYENNE PEPPER

1 TEASPOON SALT

½ CUP OLIVE OIL

3 TABLESPOONS LIME JUICE

☐ Cut the corn kernels from the cobs. Put them in a bowl with the lima beans.

☐ In a small bowl, mix the coriander or parsley, pepper, salt, oil, and lime juice.

☐ Pour over the vegetables and mix well.

YIELDS 6 SERVINGS.

Grated Carrot Salad

INGREDIENTS:

1 POUND CARROTS, GRATED

1 ORANGE

1 LEMON

½ CUP OLIVE OIL

2 TABLESPOONS MINCED PARSLEY

☐ Grate the carrots and put them in a bowl.

☐ Remove the orange zest from the orange without cutting into the white pith. Cut the zest into very thin strips and blanch in boiling water for 4 minutes. Drain. Add to the carrots.

☐ Squeeze the juice from the orange and the lemon into a small bowl and mix with the olive oil and parsley.

☐ Pour the dressing over the carrots and toss gently.

YIELDS 4 TO 6 SERVINGS.

Salade Pompadour
Cauliflower and Bean Salad

☐ Rinse the beans under cold water, drain, and put into a bowl. Add the eggs to the beans.

☐ In a bowl, toss the potatoes with the vinegar and wine.

☐ Season the mayonnaise with mustard to taste.

☐ Add the potatoes to the beans, along with the cauliflower.

☐ Add just enough seasoned mayonnaise to bind the salad.

☐ Serve on lettuce leaves.

YIELDS 4 TO 6 SERVINGS.

INGREDIENTS:
2 CUPS CANNED WHITE BEANS, DRAINED
2 HARD-COOKED EGGS, SLICED
1 CUP DICED COOKED POTATOES
2 TABLESPOONS TARRAGON VINEGAR
2 TABLESPOONS DRY WHITE WINE
1 SMALL CAULIFLOWER, COOKED
MAYONNAISE, SEE PAGE 178
DIJON MUSTARD TO TASTE
LETTUCE LEAVES

Salade de Pois Chiches
Chick Pea Salad

☐ Drain the chick peas in a sieve, rinse under cold water, and drain again.

☐ In a bowl, combine the garlic, vinegar, pepper, and olive oil, and whisk together. Add the chick peas, olives, and salami, and toss gently. Let marinate for at least 30 minutes.

☐ Arrange some salad greens on a platter. Top with the chick pea salad and sprinkle with the scallions.

☐ Place the tomatoes around the edge and sprinkle with minced parsley.

YIELDS 4 SERVINGS.

INGREDIENTS:
1-POUND CAN CHICK PEAS
1 CLOVE GARLIC, CRUSHED
½ TABLESPOON TARRAGON VINEGAR
PEPPER TO TASTE
¼ CUP OLIVE OIL
½ CUP STUFFED OLIVES, SLICED
¼ POUND GENOA SALAMI, CUT INTO STRIPS
SALAD GREENS
3 TABLESPOONS MINCED SCALLIONS
2 TOMATOES, QUARTERED
2 TABLESPOONS MINCED PARSLEY

Oriental Sweet and Sour Cucumber Salad

INGREDIENTS:
1½ POUNDS CUCUMBERS
2 TEASPOONS SALT
2 HOT PEPPERS, THINLY
  SLICED
3 TABLESPOONS RICE
  VINEGAR
3 TABLESPOONS SUGAR
2½ TABLESPOONS SOY SAUCE
2 TEASPOONS SESAME OIL

☐ Cut the cucumbers into ¼-inch-thick slices. Toss with the salt and let drain for 30 minutes.

☐ Discard any seeds from the hot peppers.

☐ In a bowl, stir the vinegar, sugar, and soy sauce until the sugar is dissolved.

☐ Heat a large skillet or wok until very hot and add the sesame oil. When it is hot, stir fry the peppers for 10 seconds. Add the cucumbers and stir fry for 1 minute.

☐ Add the vinegar mixture to the skillet and toss again. Remove the skillet from the heat and let cool. Serve at room temperature.

YIELDS 4 TO 6 SERVINGS.

Cucumber and Potato Salad

INGREDIENTS:
1 POUND CUCUMBERS,
  PEELED
1 POUND NEW POTATOES
½ CUP MINT LEAVES,
  CHOPPED
½ CUP ALMONDS, BLANCHED
½ CUP OLIVE OIL
2 TABLESPOONS LEMON
  JUICE OR TO TASTE
SALT AND PEPPER TO TASTE

☐ Cut the cucumbers in half lengthwise, remove the seeds, and cut into thin slices. Soak in a bowl of salted cold water for 30 minutes. Drain, rinse, and dry.

☐ In boiling salted water, cook the potatoes until just tender. Peel, let cool, and slice as thickly as the cucumbers.

☐ In a bowl, combine the cucumbers, potatoes, mint leaves, and almonds.

☐ In a small bowl, mix together the oil, lemon juice, salt, and pepper. Fold into the salad.

YIELDS 4 TO 6 SERVINGS.

Potatoes Romagna

☐ Put the potatoes into a bowl of water with the lemon juice.

☐ Cook the potatoes in boiling salted water for 3 minutes, stirring gently with a wooden spoon. The potatoes should still be crisp. Drain, rinse under cold water, and drain again.

☐ In a bowl, combine the potatoes with the cheese.

☐ In a small bowl, add salt, pepper, and cayenne to the chives and mayonnaise. Fold into the potato mixture.

☐ Turn the potatoes into a serving dish and garnish with the prosciutto and mushrooms.

YIELDS 4 TO 6 SERVINGS.

INGREDIENTS:

3 POTATOES, CUT INTO JULIENNE

JUICE OF 1 LEMON

½ POUND FONTINA, CUT INTO JULIENNE

SALT AND PEPPER TO TASTE

⅛ TEASPOON CAYENNE PEPPER

1 TABLESPOON MINCED CHIVES

¾ CUP MAYONNAISE, SEE PAGE 178

2 OUNCES PROSCIUTTO, CHOPPED

2 MUSHROOM CAPS, SLICED

Chef's Rice Salad

Tongue may not be readily available in many ports. Feel free to substitute salami, chicken, or turkey, cut into strips.

☐ Mix the rice with the tongue, ham, tomato, mushrooms, scallions, and basil.

☐ In a small bowl, combine the olive oil, vinegar, and salt and pepper. Pour over the salad and toss gently.

☐ Serve on a bed of lettuce leaves, if desired.

YIELDS 4 SERVINGS.

INGREDIENTS:

1 CUP RICE, COOKED, DRAINED, AND COOLED

1 CUP TONGUE, CUT INTO JULIENNE

1 CUP HAM, CUT INTO JULIENNE

1 TOMATO, PEELED, SEEDED, AND CHOPPED

6 MUSHROOMS, CHOPPED

½ CUP CHOPPED SCALLIONS

1 TABLESPOON MINCED BASIL

¼ CUP OLIVE OIL

2 TABLESPOONS VINEGAR

SALT AND PEPPER TO TASTE

LETTUCE LEAVES (OPTIONAL)

Rice Salad I

INGREDIENTS:

2 CUPS RICE, COOKED AND COOLED

3 TO 4 TABLESPOONS OLIVE OIL

SALT AND PEPPER TO TASTE

1 GREEN PEPPER, MINCED

1 SPANISH ONION, MINCED

1 TOMATO, PEELED AND CHOPPED

¼ CUP MINCED PARSLEY

¼ CUP MINCED BASIL

1 CUP MAYONNAISE, SEE PAGE 178

☐ When the rice has cooled, toss with the olive oil, salt and pepper, green pepper, onion, tomato, parsley, and basil. Chill.

☐ Shortly before serving, correct the seasoning, adding more oil, salt, and pepper as desired.

☐ Serve the mayonnaise on the side.

YIELDS 6 SERVINGS.

Rice Salad II

INGREDIENTS:

1 CUP RICE, COOKED, DRAINED, AND COOLED

6 OUNCES ANCHOVY FILLETS, DRAINED AND CHOPPED

1 CUP MINCED SCALLIONS

1 CUP MINCED PIMIENTO

2 TOMATOES, IN ¼-INCH DICE

¼ CUP RED WINE VINEGAR

1 TEASPOON DRY MUSTARD

SALT AND PEPPER TO TASTE

¾ CUP OLIVE OIL

☐ In a bowl, combine the rice, anchovies, scallions, pimiento, and tomatoes. Toss gently but thoroughly.

☐ In a small bowl, beat the vinegar, mustard, salt, and pepper and gradually beat in the olive oil until the mixture is smooth and thick. Correct seasoning with salt and pepper and pour over the salad. Toss well.

☐ Arrange in a serving bowl. For a more elaborate presentation, pack into a mold (a mixing bowl will do), chill for 2 hours, and unmold onto a bed of lettuce leaves.

YIELDS 4 TO 6 SERVINGS.

Rice Salad III

☐ In a bowl, combine the vinaigrette and mayonnaise.

☐ Toss the rice with the mixture, and fold in the radishes, green pepper, gherkins, chives, dill, and parsley.

☐ Correct seasoning with salt and pepper.

YIELDS 6 SERVINGS.

INGREDIENTS:

¾ CUP VINAIGRETTE, SEE PAGE 178

¼ CUP MAYONNAISE, SEE PAGE 178

1½ CUPS RICE, COOKED, DRAINED, AND COOLED

½ CUP RADISHES, THINLY SLICED

1 GREEN PEPPER, MINCED

2 TABLESPOONS MINCED GHERKINS

1 TABLESPOON MINCED CHIVES

1 TABLESPOON MINCED DILL

1 TABLESPOON PARSLEY, MINCED

SALT AND PEPPER TO TASTE

Salade de Riz Derby
Rice Salad Derby

☐ In a bowl, mix the rice, peas, mushrooms, and ham.

☐ In another bowl, mix the vinaigrette and mayonnaise.

☐ Add to the rice and toss gently. Add more dressing if desired.

☐ Mound onto a platter and sprinkle with walnuts.

YIELDS 4 TO 6 SERVINGS.

INGREDIENTS:

2 CUPS COLD COOKED RICE

⅔ CUP COLD COOKED PEAS

⅔ CUP MUSHROOMS, CUT INTO JULIENNE

⅔ CUP HAM, CUT INTO JULIENNE

6 TABLESPOONS VINAIGRETTE, SEE PAGE 178

2 TABLESPOONS MAYONNAISE, SEE PAGE 178

½ CUP CHOPPED WALNUTS

Portugiesischer Salat

Portuguese Salad

INGREDIENTS:

1½ CUPS MUSHROOMS, SLICED

1½ CUPS COOKED POTATOES, SLICED

1½ CUPS SLICED TOMATOES

½ CUP PITTED RIPE OLIVES

1½ CUPS VINAIGRETTE, SEE PAGE 178

☐ In a bowl, fold the mushrooms, potatoes, tomatoes, and olives with the vinaigrette. Let marinate for at least 30 minutes before serving.

YIELDS 6 SERVINGS.

Ginger-Apricot Rice Salad

INGREDIENTS:

1½ CUPS RICE

1-INCH PIECE OF GINGERROOT

BLACK PEPPER TO TASTE

NUTMEG TO TASTE

½ TEASPOON GROUND CORIANDER

1 TABLESPOON LEMON JUICE

1 SHALLOT, THINLY SLICED

½ CUP OLIVE OIL

½ CUP RAISINS

½ CUP CURRANTS

4 FRESH OR DRIED APRICOTS

4 TABLESPOONS TOASTED SLIVERED ALMONDS

☐ In a large pot, boil the rice and gingerroot in plenty of salted water for 12 to 15 minutes or until just barely tender. Drain carefully, rinse under cold water, and drain again.

☐ While the rice is still warm, season it with pepper, nutmeg, coriander, lemon juice, and shallot.

☐ Stir in just enough oil to make the rice moist but not mushy.

☐ Blanch the raisins and currants in boiling water for 2 minutes, drain, and fold into the rice.

☐ Dice the apricots and add to the rice. If they are dried, soak in hot water for 30 minutes or until tender. Fold together.

☐ Arrange in a serving dish and sprinkle with the almonds.

YIELDS 6 SERVINGS.

Tomatoes Stuffed with Rice and Cheese

☐ Cut the tops off the tomatoes, seed, and scoop out the pulp. Reserve.

☐ Sprinkle the insides with a little salt and allow to drain.

☐ Sauté the shallots and garlic in 1½ tablespoons of the olive oil for 2 minutes.

☐ Add the rice, stir, and add the wine. Reduce until almost dry.

☐ Add the stock and simmer, partially covered, until rice is cooked but quite firm. Pour the rice into a bowl and let it cool.

☐ Chop the tomato pulp coarsely and fold it into the rice.

☐ Toss the rice with two-thirds of the basil, the mozzarella, salt, pepper, and lemon juice. Stuff the tomato shells.

☐ Sprinkle reserved basil and Parmesan over the top.

INGREDIENTS:
4 LARGE TOMATOES
2½ TABLESPOONS OLIVE OIL
¼ CUP CHOPPED SHALLOTS
1 CLOVE GARLIC, MINCED
½ CUP RICE
1 TABLESPOON DRY WHITE WINE
¼ CUP CHICKEN STOCK
¼ CUP MINCED BASIL
4 OUNCES MOZZARELLA, IN ¼-INCH CUBES
SALT AND PEPPER TO TASTE
1 TABLESPOON LEMON JUICE
⅓ CUP GRATED PARMESAN

YIELDS 4 SERVINGS.

Tomatoes with Basil

☐ Arrange the tomatoes on a serving platter and sprinkle with vinaigrette and basil. To vary the flavor, arrange thin slices of mozzarella, young Parmesan, or hard ricotta between the slices of tomatoes.

☐ Let marinate for at least 1 hour, basting with juices.

INGREDIENTS:
4 TOMATOES SLICED
⅓ CUP VINAIGRETTE, SEE PAGE 178
MINCED FRESH BASIL

YIELDS 4 SERVINGS.

Zucchini and Summer Squash Salad

INGREDIENTS:
2 ONIONS, THINLY SLICED
1 GARLIC CLOVE, CRUSHED
¼ CUP OLIVE OIL
12 OUNCES ZUCCHINI,
  QUARTERED AND SLICED
12 OUNCES SUMMER SQUASH,
  QUARTERED AND SLICED
1 TOMATO, PEELED, SEEDED,
  AND CUT INTO EIGHTHS
10 OIL-CURED OLIVES,
  PITTED
1 TABLESPOON MINCED
  PARSLEY
SALT AND PEPPER TO TASTE
LEMON JUICE

☐ In a skillet, sauté the onion and garlic in the olive oil over low heat until soft but not brown.

☐ Stir in the zucchini and summer squash and cook over low heat until tender but still firm.

☐ Stir in the tomatoes, olives, parsley, salt, and pepper, and transfer to a bowl. Let cool.

☐ Fold in the lemon juice.

YIELDS 5 TO 6 SERVINGS.

Salade Jacques

INGREDIENTS:
1 POUND BELGIAN ENDIVES,
  IN ¾-INCH SLIVERS
5 TABLESPOONS RAISINS
5 TABLESPOONS CHOPPED
  WALNUTS
5 TABLESPOONS GREEK
  OLIVES, HALVED
5 TABLESPOONS DICED
  GRUYÈRE
5 TABLESPOONS CHOPPED
  APPLE
3 TO 4 TABLESPOONS GENOA
  SALAMI, CHOPPED
1 TABLESPOON MINCED
  ONION
½ CUP OLIVE OIL
½ TEASPOON DRY MUSTARD
½ CUP VINEGAR
½ TEASPOON WORCESTER-
  SHIRE SAUCE
SALT AND PEPPER TO TASTE

☐ In a bowl, mix the endives, raisins, walnuts, olives, Gruyère, apple, salami, and onion.

☐ In a small bowl, beat the olive oil, mustard, vinegar, Worcestershire sauce, salt, and pepper.

☐ Pour the dressing over the salad and toss to mix.

YIELDS 4 SERVINGS.

Tuna, Onion, and Bean Salad

☐ Drain the oil from the tuna fish and flake it into a bowl.

☐ Rinse the cannelloni beans under cold water and drain again. Add them to the tuna along with the onions. Season with salt and pepper.

☐ Add enough oil to coat the beans and tuna well, and add about ¼ as much of the vinegar as you did oil. Toss together gently.

☐ Let marinate for 1 hour.

YIELDS 4 SERVINGS.

INGREDIENTS:

2 7-OUNCE CANS TUNA PACKED IN OLIVE OIL

11-OUNCE CAN CANNELLONI BEANS, DRAINED

2 MILD ONIONS, THINLY SLICED

SALT AND PEPPER TO TASTE

½ TO ¾ CUP OLIVE OIL

2 TO 4 TABLESPOONS VINEGAR

Cold Stuffed Tomatoes

☐ Cut the tops off the tomatoes, scoop out the insides, and discard. Season the insides of the tomato shells with salt and turn them over to drain.

☐ Broil the eggplants, turning often, until the skin is charred on all sides. Take care not to pierce the skin. Cut the eggplants in half lengthwise, scoop out the pulp, and place it in a small strainer. Sprinkle the pulp with salt and let it drain for 30 minutes. Chop the eggplant.

☐ In a bowl, mix the eggplant with garlic, chives, parsley, and mayonnaise.

☐ Correct the seasoning with salt and pepper and chill for 30 minutes.

☐ Fill the tomato shells with the eggplant mixture and garnish with olives and pimiento.

YIELDS 6 SERVINGS.

INGREDIENTS:

6 TOMATOES

SALT AND PEPPER TO TASTE

2 MEDIUM EGGPLANTS

2 GARLIC CLOVES, CRUSHED

2 TABLESPOONS MINCED CHIVES

2 TABLESPOONS MINCED PARSLEY

3 TABLESPOONS MAYONNAISE, SEE PAGE 178

8 GREEK OLIVES

PIMIENTO STRIPS

Mediterranean Fish Salad

INGREDIENTS:

2 POUNDS WHITE FISH
    FILLETS, CUT INTO ½-INCH
    STRIPS
1 QUART BOILING WATER
1 ONION, SLICED
½ CUP PITTED RIPE OLIVES,
    SLICED
¼ CUP OLIVE OIL
2 TABLESPOONS RED WINE
    VINEGAR
1 TABLESPOON LIME JUICE
½ TEASPOON SALT
½ TEASPOON GROUND
    CUMIN
⅛ TEASPOON CAYENNE
    PEPPER
PINCH OF BLACK PEPPER
2 BAY LEAVES, CRUMBLED
1 ORANGE, THINLY SLICED

□ Place the fish in boiling water and return to the boil. Remove from heat, let stand 10 minutes, and drain.

□ In a bowl, beat the onion, olives, olive oil, vinegar, lime juice, salt, cumin, cayenne, black pepper, and bay leaf.

□ Carefully add the fish and fold to coat with the mixture. Refrigerate, covered, stirring occasionally.

□ Arrange on a serving dish and surround with orange slices.

YIELDS 4 SERVINGS.

Cabillaud à la Moutarde
Cod with Mustard Sauce

You can, of course, substitute any fish of your choice for the cod.

INGREDIENTS:

JUICE OF 1 LEMON
3 PARSLEY SPRIGS
SINGLE PIECE OF 2-POUND
    COD
6 LEMON WEDGES
PARSLEY FOR GARNISH
½ CUP CRÈME DE
    MOUTARDE, SEE FACING
    PAGE

□ In a flat pan, combine the lemon juice, parsley sprigs, and enough water to just cover the cod. Bring the liquid to a boil, then lower the heat, and poach the cod, simmering gently for 10 to 15 minutes or until done. Remove from heat and let the cod cool in the pan.

□ When you are ready to serve, drain the cod, arrange it on a platter, and garnish with lemon wedges and parsley.

□ Pour a strip of sauce over the fish and pass additional sauce if desired.

YIELDS 6 SERVINGS.

Crème de Moutarde
Mustard Cream Dressing

☐ In a bowl, beat the cream until it forms soft peaks.

☐ Beat in the mustard.

☐ Correct the seasoning with salt and pepper.

YIELDS ½ CUP.

INGREDIENTS:
½ CUP HEAVY CREAM
1 TABLESPOON DIJON
   MUSTARD
SALT AND PEPPER TO TASTE

Kasesalata
Cheese Salad

☐ In a bowl, mix the celery and beets together and bind with the mayonnaise. Correct seasoning with salt and pepper.

☐ Arrange the lettuce leaves on a platter, mound the vegetables in the center, and garnish with the cheese, hard-cooked egg slices, and anchovy fillets.

YIELDS 4 TO 6 SERVINGS.

INGREDIENTS:
2 CUPS CHOPPED CELERY
2 CUPS CHOPPED BEETS
½ CUP MAYONNAISE, SEE
   PAGE 178
SALT AND PEPPER TO TASTE
LETTUCE LEAVES
1½ CUPS COARSELY GRATED
   GRUYÈRE
2 HARD-COOKED EGGS,
   SLICED
1 CAN ROLLED ANCHOVY
   FILLETS

Zucchini Salad

☐ Sauté the zucchini in the butter and oil until just tender.

☐ Cool in a bowl and toss with the vinaigrette, parsley, and garlic.

YIELDS 2 SERVINGS.

INGREDIENTS:
1 POUND SMALL ZUCCHINI,
   THINLY SLICED
2 TABLESPOONS BUTTER
2 TABLESPOONS OLIVE OIL
½ CUP VINAIGRETTE, SEE
   PAGE 178
1 TEASPOON MINCED PARSLEY
½ TEASPOON MINCED GARLIC

Shrimp in Tomato-Caper Mayonnaise

This recipe is also delicious with lobster meat, crab, or scallops. Poached whitefish such as cod, sole, or halibut also work well.

INGREDIENTS:
1 POUND SHRIMP, PEELED
2 TABLESPOONS OLIVE OIL
¼ CUP MINCED PARSLEY
1 SHALLOT, MINCED
1 TOMATO, PEELED, SEEDED, AND CHOPPED
1 TEASPOON MINCED BASIL
2 TABLESPOONS CAPERS, DRAINED
1 CUP MAYONNAISE, SEE PAGE 178
LETTUCE LEAVES

☐ In a skillet, sauté the shrimp in the oil until they just turn pink. Drain and let cool.

☐ In a bowl, mix together the parsley, shallot, tomato, basil, capers, and mayonnaise.

☐ Add the shrimp and mix gently.

☐ Arrange the lettuce leaves on a plate and fill with shrimp.

YIELDS 4 SERVINGS.

Salade Argentine
Green Bean and Flank Steak Salad

INGREDIENTS:
1 POUND GREEN BEANS, TRIMMED
2 POUNDS FLANK STEAK, COOKED
1½ TABLESPOONS RED WINE VINEGAR
6 TABLESPOONS OLIVE OIL
3 TABLESPOONS LEMON JUICE
SALT AND PEPPER TO TASTE
4 TABLESPOONS SOUR CREAM
2 TABLESPOONS DIJON MUSTARD
MINCED PARSLEY

☐ Cook the beans in boiling salted water until tender but still crisp. Cool in cold water. Drain.

☐ Slice the cooled cooked steak in very thin strips across the grain. Add to the green beans in a bowl.

☐ In a small bowl, mix the red wine vinegar, olive oil, lemon juice, salt, pepper, sour cream, and mustard. Pour the dressing over the beans and steak, toss gently, and arrange on a serving dish. Sprinkle with parsley.

YIELDS 6 SERVINGS.

TEN

DESSERTS

If your idea of dessert is apple pie, chocolate cake, or cream puffs, you will find your choices limited at sea. However, there are desserts that can be prepared in a galley with little effort. I recommend fresh fruit, served plain or as a fruit salad, or flavored with a liqueur. For the most part, canned and frozen fruits are not very good and truly should be avoided. The fruits' texture changes during processing and color is often lost. Luckily, the sailing season is also the season for fresh fruits and you can get a good selection at whatever ports you hit.

Cookies are a wonderful accompaniment to fruits. If you have time to prepare some of those listed here, pack them in airtight containers to bring along. Packaged cookies generally do not taste very good. Of course, if there is a brand that pleases you, bring it along. You can make a cake or pie to bring along, but I would be hard pressed to produce such a thing on a boat. I leave the baking till I get home.

If you feel that you cannot live without baked goods, check out each port to see if it does not have a decent bake shop where you can purchase what you like. At any rate, try some of the fruit recipes here. You might not realize until much later that you went through a week or more without baked goods. If you bring wine on board, as I always do, you will find that the most satisfying dessert consists of fruit, cheese, and red wine.

Sautéed Fruits

One of the easiest and nicest desserts is to sauté the fruit of your choice in a little butter. You can enhance the flavor with a complementing liqueur or a splash of cream.

INGREDIENTS:
2 TO 3 CUPS FRUIT
2 TABLESPOONS BUTTER
6 TABLESPOONS SUGAR
JUICE OF 2 ORANGES
2 TABLESPOONS GRAND
 MARNIER
½ TO 1 CUP HEAVY CREAM

☐ Prepare the fruit according to its type. Hull strawberries and slice them if they are large. Peel and cut bananas into halves lengthwise or crosswise, slice peaches into wedges, cut apples into wedges or rings. Peel pineapple and cut into rings or sticks, etc.

☐ In a skillet, heat the butter until melted, add the sugar, and cook until it starts to turn golden.

☐ Add the fruit and cook until heated through and browned. Serve immediately.

☐ Another option is to prepare the following sauce for the fruit. Stir in the orange juice and reduce by half. Add the Grand Marnier and heat through. Add the cream, cook it to a saucelike consistency, and pour over the sautéed fruit.

Note: The liqueur can be changed to one of your choice. Try Cognac or bourbon with peaches, rum with pineapple, etc.

YIELDS 4 SERVINGS.

Fruits in Liqueur

Try peaches in bourbon, strawberries in Cognac, pineapple in orange liqueur or Pernod, etc.

INGREDIENTS:
2 TO 3 CUPS FRUIT, CUT UP
LIQUEUR OF YOUR CHOICE

☐ Place the fruit in a bowl, sprinkle with liqueur, and let stand for 15 minutes to develop the flavor.

☐ Add sugar to taste if necessary.

YIELDS 4 TO 6 SERVINGS.

Fruits in Cream

☐ Cut the fruit as indicated in the previous recipe. Blueberries need only to be rinsed and picked over, as do raspberries. Cherries should be pitted, but if you give people fair warning, you can skip the step.

☐ Sweeten the fruit with sugar to taste and let stand at least 20 minutes. At this point you may also flavor the fruit with a liqueur – cherries with kirsch, blueberries with orange liqueur and a little grated lemon rind, etc.

☐ Beat the cream until stiff, fold into the fruit, and serve. Or pour plain cream over the fruit and serve.

INGREDIENTS:
2 TO 3 CUPS FRUIT
SUGAR TO TASTE
1 CUP HEAVY CREAM
LIQUEUR OF YOUR CHOICE

YIELDS 4 SERVINGS.

Arance Tagliate
Sliced Oranges

☐ Peel 4 oranges and cut into thin slices, picking out and discarding any seeds.

☐ Put the orange into a serving bowl and top with lemon peel and sugar.

☐ Squeeze the juice from the remaining oranges and add it to the bowl with the lemon juice. (Add a couple of tablespoons of maraschino or orange liqueur, if you like.) Toss gently.

☐ Refrigerate until serving time.

INGREDIENTS:
6 ORANGES
GRATED PEEL OF 1 LEMON
5 TABLESPOONS SUGAR
JUICE OF ½ LEMON

YIELDS 4 SERVINGS.

Mixed Fruits in Sour Cream

Try various mixtures: strawberries and blueberries; pineapple, strawberries, and oranges; oranges and bananas, etc.

INGREDIENTS:
2 TO 3 CUPS MIXED FRUITS
½ CUP SOUR CREAM
¼ CUP BROWN SUGAR

☐ In a bowl, toss the fruits together gently, fold in the sour cream, and sprinkle with the brown sugar.

☐ Let stand for 15 minutes in a cool place.

YIELDS 4 TO 6 SERVINGS.

Gingered Blueberry Compote

INGREDIENTS:
1 PINT BLUEBERRIES, WASHED
1 CUP ORANGE JUICE
¼ CUP SUGAR
2 TABLESPOONS MINCED
   PRESERVED GINGER
MINT LEAVES

☐ Place the berries in a bowl and sprinkle with the orange juice, sugar, and ginger. Toss gently and garnish with the mint.

YIELDS 4 SERVINGS.

Pickled Strawberries

This may sound odd, but it is wonderful. Try it.

INGREDIENTS:
1 QUART STRAWBERRIES,
   SLICED
2 TABLESPOONS SUGAR
PINCH OF CINNAMON
2 TEASPOONS BALSAMIC
   VINEGAR
1 BOTTLE OF DRY
   SPARKLING WINE

☐ In a bowl combine the strawberries, sugar and cinnamon.

☐ Let stand for 30 minutes, turning occasionally.

☐ Sprinkle with vinegar and toss.

☐ Refrigerate covered until serving time.

☐ Divide among serving dishes and pour on the wine.

YIELDS 4 TO 8 SERVINGS.

Cherries in Sour Cream

☐ Place the cherries in a bowl and mix with the kirsch.

☐ Fold in the sour cream, sugar, and cinnamon. Toss gently. Chill if possible.

☐ Sprinkle the chocolate over the top.

YIELDS 4 SERVINGS.

INGREDIENTS:
2 POUNDS CHERRIES, PITTED
2 OUNCES KIRSCH
1 CUP SOUR CREAM
2 TABLESPOONS SUGAR
1 TEASPOON CINNAMON
GRATED SEMI-SWEET
   CHOCOLATE

Grapes in Brandy

☐ Mix the honey, Cognac, and lemon juice in a bowl.

☐ Mix in the grapes and chill for 1 hour or longer.

☐ Top with the sour cream.

YIELDS 4 SERVINGS.

INGREDIENTS:
¼ CUP HONEY
6 TABLESPOONS COGNAC
1 TABLESPOON LEMON JUICE
1 POUND SEEDLESS GRAPES,
   WASHED
1 CUP SOUR CREAM

Poires en Cointreau
Pears in Cointreau

☐ In a serving bowl, combine the pears, sugar, Cointreau, lemon juice, and orange juice.

☐ Let stand for at least 1 hour.

YIELDS 6 SERVINGS.

INGREDIENTS:
6 PEARS, PEELED AND SLICED
1 TABLESPOON SUGAR
¼ CUP COINTREAU OR OTHER
   ORANGE LIQUEUR
1 TEASPOON LEMON JUICE
1 CUP ORANGE JUICE

Macedonia di Frutta

Mixed Fresh Fruit Compote

INGREDIENTS:

1½ CUPS ORANGE JUICE

GRATED PEEL OF 1 LEMON

3 TABLESPOONS LEMON JUICE

2 APPLES, PEELED AND
   SLICED

2 PEARS, PEELED AND SLICED

2 BANANAS, SLICED

1½ POUNDS ASSORTED
   FRUITS (GRAPES, SEEDED;
   CHERRIES, PITTED;
   APRICOTS, STONED;
   PLUMS AND PEACHES,
   STONED; MELON BALLS)

6 TABLESPOONS SUGAR OR
   TO TASTE

¼ CUP MARASCHINO
   LIQUEUR, OR OTHER
   LIQUEUR

☐ In a bowl, combine the orange juice, lemon peel, lemon juice, apples, pears, and other fruits as available. (If adding bananas or strawberries, do so shortly before serving.) Mix with the sugar and liqueur.

☐ Cover and chill for 2 hours.

YIELDS 6 SERVINGS.

Macedoine of Fruit

INGREDIENTS:

1 PINEAPPLE, PEELED, DICED

½ POUND OF PEACHES,
   PEELED, STONED, AND
   DICED

1 PINT STRAWBERRIES,
   HALVED

1 TEASPOON MINCED GINGER

1 TEASPOON GRATED
   LEMON RIND

¼ CUP PORT

SUGAR

☐ In a bowl, combine the pineapple, peaches, strawberries, ginger, and lemon rind. Toss gently and fold in the port. Add sugar if needed.

YIELDS 6 SERVINGS.

Peaches in Wine

☐ Place the peaches in a bowl, sprinkle with sugar, and pour on the wine. Allow to stand for 1 hour before serving.

YIELDS 6 SERVINGS.

INGREDIENTS:

6 LARGE PEACHES, PEELED, STONED, AND SLICED

½ TO 1 CUP RED WINE

1 TO 2 TABLESPOONS SUGAR

Peppered Strawberries

☐ In a bowl mix the strawberries and wine. Sprinkle generously with freshly ground black pepper.

YIELDS 4 SERVINGS.

INGREDIENTS:

1 QUART STRAWBERRIES, SLICED

1 CUP RED WINE

BLACK PEPPER

Strawberries in Liqueurs

☐ Place the strawberries in a bowl and toss gently with the sugar. Let stand for 10 minutes or until the sugar is dissolved.

☐ Pour on the Cointreau, kirsch, and Cognac and mix carefully.

☐ Let stand, refrigerated, for 2 hours.

☐ Serve over slices of sponge cake, garnished with whipped cream.

YIELDS 6 SERVINGS.

INGREDIENTS:

1 QUART STRAWBERRIES, SLICED

½ CUP SUGAR

1 TABLESPOON COINTREAU

1 TABLESPOON KIRSCH

2 TABLESPOONS COGNAC

6 SLICES SPONGE CAKE (OPTIONAL)

1 CUP HEAVY CREAM, WHIPPED

Fragole al Limone

Strawberries with Lemon

INGREDIENTS:
1½ QUARTS STRAWBERRIES
SUGAR TO TASTE
JUICE OF 2 LEMONS

☐ Hull strawberries and crush ½ cup of them.

☐ Put the whole strawberries in a bowl with the strawberry pulp, sugar, and lemon juice.

☐ Mix and let stand for 30 minutes.

YIELDS 6 SERVINGS.

Butter Almond Cake

INGREDIENTS:
⅔ CUP BUTTER
1 CUP ALMOND PASTE
1 CUP SUGAR
4 EGGS
GRATED ZEST OF 1 ORANGE
⅔ CUP FLOUR
PINCH OF SALT
½ TEASPOON BAKING
  POWDER
1 CUP SLICED ALMONDS

☐ Preheat the oven to 350°F.

☐ Butter a 9-inch-square baking pan and dust with flour.

☐ Cream the butter and almond paste until well combined. Gradually beat in the sugar until light and fluffy.

☐ Add the eggs, one at a time, and blend in the orange zest.

☐ In a bowl, mix the flour, salt, and baking powder, and blend into the batter. Pour the batter into the pan, and arrange the almonds in diagonal lines over the surface.

☐ Bake until golden, about 40 minutes.

☐ Remove from the oven and let cool for 5 minutes in the pan.

☐ Turn onto a rack, turn right side up and cool.

☐ Cut into 1-inch pieces.

YIELDS 81 SQUARES.

Melon Oranges and Blueberries

□ In a bowl, combine the honeydew, orange juice, liqueur, sugar, and orange peel.

□ Toss gently and chill covered for 3 hours.

□ Fold in the blueberries and serve.

YIELDS 4 TO 6 SERVINGS.

INGREDIENTS:

1 HONEYDEW CUT INTO BALLS OR CUBES

¾ CUP ORANGE JUICE

¼ CUP ORANGE-FLAVORED LIQUEUR

2 TABLESPOONS SUGAR

2 TEASPOONS GRATED ORANGE PEEL

1 PINT BLUEBERRIES

Shortbread Cookies

□ Preheat the oven to 300°F.

□ In a processor, mix the flour, butter, cornstarch, and sugar until blended, about 30 seconds. Refrigerate 1 hour until firm enough to handle.

□ Shape into 1-inch balls and place on unbuttered baking sheets. Flatten each ball with a lightly floured fork, leaving a crisscross pattern.

□ Bake for 10 minutes or until edges are just lightly browned.

INGREDIENTS:

1 CUP FLOUR

¾ CUP BUTTER

½ CUP CORNSTARCH

1 CUP CONFECTIONERS' SUGAR

Note: Another method of forming the cookies would be to turn the mixture onto a sheet of waxed paper and shape it into a log about 1½ inches in diameter. Chill until firm and cut into ¼-inch-thick slices.

YIELDS ABOUT 36 COOKIES.

Bangor Brownies

INGREDIENTS:

2 OUNCES UNSWEETENED
  CHOCOLATE
¼ CUP MELTED BUTTER
1 CUP SUGAR
1 EGG
1½ CUPS FLOUR
½ TEASPOON SALT
½ CUP CHOPPED NUTS

☐ Preheat the oven to 350°F.

☐ Butter an 8-inch-square baking pan.

☐ Melt the chocolate in a double boiler, and stir in the butter, sugar, and the egg.

☐ Mix the flour and salt together and stir into the chocolate mixture with the nuts.

☐ Pour into the pan and bake 25 minutes.

☐ The brownies will be very soft but will harden as they cool.

YIELDS 16 BROWNIES.

Ciambellette
Jelly Cookies

Use any jam or jelly of your choice. Apricot, currant, and raspberry are the more traditional flavors.

INGREDIENTS:

½ CUP BUTTER
½ CUP SUGAR
2 EGG YOLKS
1 TEASPOON ALMOND
  EXTRACT
1 CUP FLOUR
½ CUP CORNSTARCH
JELLY OR PRESERVES

☐ Preheat the oven to 375°F.

☐ Butter a cookie sheet.

☐ In a processor, cream the butter and sugar until fluffy.

☐ Add the egg, almond extract, and flour, which has been mixed with cornstarch. The dough should be relatively stiff.

☐ Roll into ¾-inch balls and place on cookie sheets. Press down in the center with your finger. The sides do split but that is all right.

☐ Fill each indentation with a dab of jelly.

☐ Bake for 12 to 15 minutes or until very lightly colored.

YIELDS ABOUT 36 COOKIES.

Butter Tart Squares

☐ Preheat the oven to 350°F.

☐ In a bowl, cream the butter and add 1 cup of flour and sugar. Blend until smooth.

☐ Transfer to a 9-inch-square baking dish, spreading evenly.

☐ Bake until lightly browned, about 15 minutes. Set aside.

☐ In a bowl, mix the brown sugar, eggs, remaining flour, vanilla, and baking powder. Stir in the raisins and nuts.

☐ Spread over the crust and bake until golden, about 30 minutes.

☐ Cool and cut into squares.

YIELDS ABOUT 36 1– by 3–INCH RECTANGLES.

INGREDIENTS:
½ CUP BUTTER
1 CUP SIFTED FLOUR
2 TABLESPOONS SUGAR
1½ CUPS PACKED BROWN SUGAR
2 EGGS
2 TABLESPOONS FLOUR
1 TEASPOON VANILLA
½ TEASPOON BAKING POWDER
1 CUP PLUMPED RAISINS
¼ CUP CHOPPED WALNUTS

ELEVEN

BASIC SAUCES AND PREPARATIONS

Every cookbook has a few basic sauces and preparations that are used in several different ways. In some instances, however, a preparation may be so frequently associated with one type of food that it is listed only there. That does not mean it cannot be used with another dish. Chicken Portuguese, for example, is a classic dish, but there is no reason that you cannot make it with fish, beef, pork, lamb, or veal. Always feel free to consider, at least, exchanging one principal ingredient for another.

Certain recipes are so basic that we can assume everyone knows them, yet we all occasionally need a reminder. Vinaigrette is something that most cooks put together without a second thought, but there are those days when the mind goes blank or when a little inspiration would be welcome.

Then there are the recipes for things (like mayonnaise) that some people always assume come out of a jar. Instead, try making your own. Mayonnaise is a simple preparation and should be in every cook's repertoire. Try it and its variations here.

COMPOSED BUTTERS

One of the simplest sauces for broiled or poached meats is a composed butter. There are dozens, some of which, such as lobster butter, require considerable work. For shipboard eating consider the simpler versions.

Basic Composed Butter

The herbs are best if fresh. Dried herbs are not as delicious. If desired, add a bit of vinegar instead of lemon juice. For texture and flavor you can work in a tablespoon of finely minced shallot.

☐ In a bowl, mash the butter until light and fluffy. Beat in the lemon juice drop by drop and then work in the herb. Season with salt and pepper.

☐ Pack into a crock to be used as a spread on bread, or shape it into a log and chill until firm. Slice the log and use on hot broiled or poached meat or fish.

INGREDIENTS:

6 TABLESPOONS BUTTER

1 TABLESPOON LEMON JUICE (OPTIONAL)

2 TABLESPOONS MINCED HERB

SALT AND PEPPER TO TASTE

YIELDS ½ CUP.

Beurre Manié
Butter Paste

This is as much an idea as it is recipe. The point is to work butter and flour together to form a paste. You can do so using either a board or a bowl. The paste is then stirred into a simmering liquid in pea-sized portions — no larger — until the sauce thickens. In Britain and the United States the closest idea is a slurry, which consists of a mixture of flour or another starch, such as cornstarch or potato starch, and water. These also are mixed into a simmering liquid to thicken it. The difference is that the Beurre manié has a richness not found in its compatriots.

For most recipes the amount listed will be more than you actually need. Use only enough to thicken the sauce lightly, until it just coats the back of a spoon. Serve as soon after the liquid has thickened as possible.

INGREDIENTS:

1 TABLESPOON BUTTER, SOFTENED

2 TABLESPOONS FLOUR

Clarified Butter

In fine cooking this is the preferred cooking fat. It has more flavor and a higher smoking point than regular butter because the milk solids have been removed. If you do not have clarified butter, or do not wish to make it, you can use an unflavored vegetable oil.

I find it easiest to cook one pound of butter at a time. It will keep for weeks.

INGREDIENTS:
1 POUND BUTTER

☐ In a small saucepan, cook the butter over low heat until it is fully melted, a crust has formed on the top, and it begins to smell nut-like.

☐ Remove from the heat and let stand for 5 minutes.

☐ Carefully spoon the crust from the top and discard.

☐ Pour the clear oil through several sheets of very fine cheesecloth or an old linen napkin. Discard the residue in the bottom of the pan.

☐ Pour the clear oil into a container and keep, covered, in the refrigerator until ready to use.

YIELDS AROUND 2 CUPS.

Vinaigrette

This sauce can be varied in many ways. Use lemon juice or lime juice in place of the vinegar for a lighter, smoother finish. If you are dressing a fruit salad, use orange juice instead of vinegar.

Use a teaspoon of dry mustard or vary the amount of Dijon mustard to taste. Add crushed garlic or minced herbs of your choice.

Try adding some chopped hard-cooked egg to the sauce to use on poached vegetables such as broccoli, green beans, or asparagus that you intend to serve as a salad, or to marinate cold cooked fish.

The basic recipe with which to experiment is as follows:

INGREDIENTS:
2 TABLESPOONS VINEGAR
2 TEASPOONS DIJON
  MUSTARD
SALT AND PEPPER TO TASTE
6 TABLESPOONS OLIVE OIL

☐ In a bowl, combine the vinegar, mustard, salt, and pepper.

☐ Gradually whisk in the oil until the mixture thickens.

YIELDS ½ CUP.

Mayonnaise

This recipe can be varied as you wish. Use Dijon mustard instead of dry. Try lemon juice instead of vinegar. To make an evenly balanced mayonnaise, I strongly recommend that you use half olive oil and half vegetable oil. Using only olive oil makes a rather heavy mayonnaise.

You can, of course, flavor the mayonnaise in countless ways. Add tomato puree or crushed tomatoes for a tomato flavor. Enhance the flavor with anchovy paste or perk it up with cayenne pepper.

Add another dimension with curry powder or add a mixture of herbs such as tarragon, chervil, chives and parsley. Rosemary for cold shellfish or thyme and marjoram for pork. Dill makes a wonderful mayonnaise for poached salmon. If desired add some peeled, seeded, diced cucumbers to this sauce. Lighten the sauce with sour cream or some whipped salted cream.

☐ In a warm bowl, mix the egg yolks, salt, mustard, and 1 teaspoon of the vinegar with a wire whisk or electric mixer until the mixture starts to thicken.

☐ Add the oil in droplets until about ¼ cup has been added.

☐ Add another teaspoon of vinegar and continue adding the oil in a slow steady stream, making sure that it is incorporated before adding more. The mayonnaise should be stiff.

☐ Season to taste with salt, pepper, and vinegar.

YIELDS ABOUT 1 CUP.

INGREDIENTS:
2 EGG YOLKS
SALT AND PEPPER TO TASTE
½ TEASPOON DRY MUSTARD
2 TABLESPOONS VINEGAR, APPROXIMATELY
1 CUP OIL, SEE ABOVE

Sauce Remoulade

This sauce is delicious in cold salads of vegetables, meat or fish. Serve to accompany plain poached fish.

☐ In a bowl, mix the mustard, lemon juice, capers, dill, parsley, garlic, egg mayonnaise, salt and cayenne pepper.

☐ Let stand 20 minutes before using.

YIELDS 2½ CUPS.

INGREDIENTS:
2 TEASPOONS DRY MUSTARD
2 TEASPOONS LEMON JUICE
1 TEASPOON CAPERS, MINCED IF LARGE
2 TABLESPOONS MINCED DILL
1 TABLESPOON MINCED PARSLEY
½ TEASPOON MINCED GARLIC
1 MINCED EGG, HARD COOKED
2 CUPS MAYONNAISE
SALT AND CAYENNE PEPPER TO TASTE

INDEX